Genealogy

DNA and the FAMILY TREE

2nd Edition

by James Mayflower

© **Copyright 2015 – James Mayflower - All rights reserved.**

In no way is it legal to reproduce, duplicate, or transmit any part of this document in either electronic means or in printed format. Recording of this publication is strictly prohibited and any storage of this document is not allowed unless with written permission from the publisher. All rights reserved.

The information provided herein is stated to be truthful and consistent, in that any liability, in terms of inattention or otherwise, by any usage or abuse of any policies, processes, or directions contained within is the solitary and utter responsibility of the recipient reader. Under no circumstances will any legal responsibility or blame be held against the publisher for any reparation, damages, or monetary loss due to the information herein, either directly or indirectly.
Respective authors own all copyrights not held by the publisher.

Legal Notice:
This book is copyright protected. This is only for personal use. You cannot amend, distribute, sell, use, quote or paraphrase any part or the content within this book without the consent of the author or copyright owner. Legal action will be pursued if this is breached.

Disclaimer Notice:
Please note the information contained within this document is for educational and entertainment purposes only. Every attempt has been made to provide accurate, up to date and reliable complete information. No warranties of any kind are

expressed or implied. Readers acknowledge that the author is not engaging in the rendering of legal, financial, medical or professional advice.

By reading this document, the reader agrees that under no circumstances are we responsible for any losses, direct or indirect, which are incurred as a result of the use of information contained within this document, including, but not limited to, —errors, omissions, or inaccuracies.

Contents

Introduction

Chapter 1: All You Need to Know About DNA

    DNA in simple Terms

    Why do we have a DNA?

    What is the structure of DNA?

    The Functions of DNA

    Where is DNA found?

Chapter 2: Genes

    Where are genes found?

    What are chromosomes?

    The connection between genes and alleles

    Mitosis

    Meiosis

Chapter 3: An Overview of Inheritance

    Concept of Inheritance

    Mendelian inheritance

    Mendel's laws of inheritance

    Non-Mendelian Inheritance

    Extra nuclear inheritance

    Gene Conversion

Infectious heredity

Genomic imprinting

Mosaicism

Trinucleotide repeat disorders

Chapter 4: A Look at the Relation Between DNA and Inheritance

The Hershey and Chase experiment

What do we get from our parents?

How do we get one chromosome from Mom and one from Dad?

Impact of parental chromosomes on offspring

Blood grouping

Dimples

Handedness

Freckles

Curly hair

Red/Green color-blindness

Hairline shape

PTC tasting

Polydactyly

Earlobe attachment

Earwax

    Cleft chin

    Lactose intolerance

    Hand clasping

Chapter 5: Everything You Need to Know About Genealogy?

    Why is Genealogy important?

    History of Genealogy

    Modern Genealogy

    Different sources of study and information

Chapter 6: A Quick Look at Genealogy and Health Ailments

    Haemophilia

    Phenylketonuria (PKU)

    Cystic fibrosis

    Albinism

    Huntington's disease

    Research in Genealogy

Chapter 7 – Online Genealogy

Chapter 8 – Where to Look For Your Ancestors

    Birth, Marriage & Death, including Parish

    Search Tips

    Census Records

    Search Tips

Immigration and Travel Information

Search Tips

UK Incoming Passenger Lists, 1878-1960

Australian Convict Transportation Registers – 1791-1868

U.S. and Canada, Passenger and Immigration Lists Index, 1500s-1900s

The New York, Passenger and Immigration Lists, 1820-1850

The UK Royal Navy Medical Journals, 1817-1857

The Slave Registers of former British Colonial Dependencies, 1813-1834

The St. Croix, U.S. Virgin Islands, Slave and Free People Records, 1733-1930

The U.S. Virgin Islands Census, 1835-1911 (Danish Period)

Military Records

WWI Records

Service records

Medal records

World War II records

Chapter 9 – Useful Advice in Searching for Your Ancestors

Ten common research mistakes

A Guide to Old Photos

Questioning Your Relatives

Top Tips for What to do When You Hit a Brick Wall

Tracing Living Relatives

Conclusion

Introduction

DNA and Genealogy may seem unrelated but, in reality, are interdependent. DNA is the biomolecule that stores all the information of an organism, which is vital for its function. The DNA not only stores information, but it is the hereditary material in almost all living beings. On the other hand, Genealogy is the science and study of family history. This study of family history can be coupled with certain concepts of DNA to help understand how certain traits are expressed in an individual or how they were inherited.

This book is divided into six chapters. Chapter one will give basic knowledge about the structure and function of a DNA molecule. The second chapter deals with genes and genetic information. The third chapter deals with the basics of inheritance and the concepts upon which inheritance may have been formed. The fourth chapter talks about how DNA is inherited by offspring from parents and about the laws of inheritance, giving examples in the form of some interesting experiments. This chapter also talks about certain traits and quirks that can be explained by that inheritance.

The fifth chapter concentrates completely on the basics of Genealogy, which include its definition, the history of Genealogy and modern Genealogy. The final chapter deals with the application of Genealogy in human health and research in the area of Genealogy. This chapter showcases a few diseases that have been passed down through generations as examples of the link mentioned between DNA and Genealogy.

All the chapters of this book are carefully designed to give readers knowledge of DNA and Genealogy and their relationship to each other. I hope you find this book informative and enlightening. I want to thank you for buying this book and I sincerely hope you enjoy it.

So without much ado, let us take a deep dive in the study of genes and DNA.

Chapter 1: All You Need to Know About DNA

DNA is a biomolecule that is responsible for producing life along with other biomolecules. It is considered as the most important biomolecule in terms of function. This is responsible for the storage of cellular information and helps to make up an individual's characteristics.

It is also known as hereditary material, as it is inherited by the offspring from their parents. Hence DNA plays an important role in making the children similar to their parents or other family members. On the other hand, Genealogy is the study of family history. It has been playing a major role in human civilization since 221BC. It also plays a major role in settling property disputes and in knowing our true ancestors. But recently it has been extensively used in medical science to determine various inheritable genetic conditions. Thus, one can see its significance.

DNA in simple Terms

Let me start this by explaining it with another question. How does anyone decide whether something is living or nonliving? Most of the people around us would say that anything that can move, eat, reproduce and die could be labeled as living. This definition stands good for a layman but might not be enough for the educated.

An educated person would say that anything that can perform, metabolize, grow, adapt, organize, respond to stimuli and die could be termed as living. On the other hand, anything that fails to perform one or more of the above mechanisms, can be termed as being nonliving.

From this, another question arises and that is what makes living things living and nonliving things non-living? The answer lies deep within the living organisms. The answer is a small molecule and, most often, it is this molecule that causes life or produces life and it is known as DNA. It is called Deoxyribonucleic acid. It has this name because of the removal of an OH group from the Ribonucleic acid that forms the basis of this biomolecule.

There exists another biomolecule that is also responsible for producing life. This is RNA or Ribonucleic acid. RNA is very similar to DNA in structure except the fact that it is single strand and DNA is made up of a double strand. This double stranded nature of DNA makes it more stable than RNA and this is why DNA is the main genetic material. There are a few viruses that use RNA as their genetic storage material. The "deoxy" part of DNA also makes it more stable than RNA.

To be more precise, it is the molecule that makes a living organism from its head to its toes.

Why do we have a DNA?

This question sounds like "Why do we need a hard disc in a computer?" Most people answer the second question by saying that it is the part of the computer that saves data. Now when we compare both computers and DNA, DNA sort of performs the same function. It is the component of the living system that stores all your biological data like your height, hair color, weight and all our external and internal (metabolic) features.

To be more precise, DNA performs more than one function in a living body. It is the storage component of the body and also the hereditary material. Wonder why some of us look alike your parents? The term hereditary means that it has the capability of passing information from one generation to the next.

What is the structure of DNA?

Before understanding the structure, one should be familiar with the components of DNA. DNA is a macromolecule (a molecule that is present in large quantities) present in all living organisms. It is a polymer (a chain containing many similar or dissimilar units) made up of many repeating units called nucleotides.

Nucleotide has three subunits; a nitrogenous base, a ribose sugar (also called pentose sugar as it has five carbons in it) and a phosphate molecule. A nucleotide without the phosphate group is called a nucleoside.

Nitrogenous bases are of two types namely purines and pyrimidines. The Purines are made of two molecules namely Adenine (denoted by an A) and Guanine (denoted by a G).

All purines are two ringed structures. Pyrimidines consist of three molecules namely Thymine (denoted by a T), Cytosine (denoted by a C) and Uracil (denoted by a U) (but only adenine, thymine, cytosine and guanine are present in DNA. Uracil is only present in RNA "Ribonucleic acid"). All pyrimidines are one-ringed structures.

Ribose sugar is a five-carbon sugar with ketose as a functional group.

Every phosphate group consists of three phosphorus atoms and ten oxygen atoms.

A nitrogenous base is connected to the ribose sugar and this ribose sugar, in turn, is connected to the phosphate group.

The beauty of DNA lies in its structure - the structure DNA was first given by Watson and Crick.

- DNA is a double helix structure (kind of a twisted ladder).
- Purines bind with pyrimidines: - adenine binds only with thymine with a double hydrogen bond. Cytosine binds with guanine with a triple hydrogen bond (hydrogen bond is a bond that is formed only between hydrogen and any other electronegative atom species like oxygen, nitrogen, chlorine etc.)
- DNA strands are antiparallel (this means one strand runs from 5' to 3' direction and the other runs from 3' to 5' direction).

    5'-------------->3'

    3'<-------------5'

It was added by other researchers that DNA comes in many forms and has many orientations.

The Functions of DNA

As discussed, DNA is vital for the survival of all living beings including plants, animals, algae, bacteria and even some viruses. It is important for inheritance of parental characteristics to offspring, making of proteins and is the genetic instruction guide for life and all its processes. DNA holds the blueprints of an organism's development, reproduction and even its death.

Although DNA can be nicknamed the master of life, it never plays a part in any of the cellular functions, but it produces another macromolecule called protein that is responsible for all cellular function. The process, through which proteins are made from DNA, is called 'central dogma' (protein synthesis).

Central dogma consists of two parts, which are known as transcription and translation. Transcription is where DNA is converted into an mRNA (messenger ribonucleic acid) and intermediate in protein synthesis. Translation is the process of turning the intermediate (mRNA) into proteins.

DNA also performs many convoluted processes and often these are thought of as miracles of nature.

Where is DNA found?

To answer this question, we need to keep dividing the organism into smaller and smaller parts. Humans, or in the sense any other organisms, are made up of organ systems. Organ systems are made up of organs. Organs are made up of tissues. Tissues are made up of cells. Cells are also the most basic unit of life, as they are self-sustaining.

When we further divide cells, we enter the sub-cellular world. As we humans have different organs for different functions, cells also have different organs different functions and these are called organelles. Cells have a variety of organelles like endoplasmic reticulum, ribosomes, nucleus etc. DNA is usually found in the nucleus in the form of chromatin.

DNA is also present in many other organelles like mitochondria of plants and animals and chloroplast of plants. The major difference between DNA found in the nucleus and in other cellular organelles is that nuclear DNA makes proteins for all other cell organelles, but DNA in mitochondria and chloroplast makes proteins only for itself.

From this, a conclusion can be obtained that DNA is found in almost all cells of the body. The word is almost always misused, as some cell-like mature red blood cells do not have a nucleus or DNA.

Chapter 2: Genes

Genes are DNA sequences that form part of chromosomes. Genes are considered to be the units of heredity by which traits are passed down from one generation to the next. Each species has a varying number of genes. This number can be anywhere from a few hundred to many thousands. Humans have about 20,000 to 25,000 genes that are found in 23 pairs of chromosomes.

These genes contain the sequences that produce code for specific proteins. These proteins are essential for the growth and functioning of the body as a whole. Proteins have various functions. Some of them are used as enzymes; some are regulators for hormones and other substances while others are structural molecules.

Where are genes found?

Almost every cell in the body has a nucleus that contains 23 pairs of chromosomes. 22 pairs are known as autosomes and the remaining one pair is known as the sex chromosome since it determines the sex of the progeny. A gene is found on all the chromosomes. It is found as a small part of a chromosome that codes a specific trait or characteristic. Genes have the ability of being switched off when they are not needed so even though an organism has thousands of genes, not all of them will be active at any given moment.

What are chromosomes?

Every cell of the human body performs its own function and helps other cells in their function. As they perform their own function they need a set of instructions to do so. DNA gives these instructions, which is present in all cells.

The average size of a human cell is 1-10 micrometers (one micrometer is hundred thousandth of a meter). Human DNA has a length of 3 meters. Therefore, it is practically impossible to fit a molecule of 3 meters into an entity of such a small size. But nature does this job well and has been doing this for a long time. The trick behind the scenes is that though DNA is very long in terms of length, it has an extremely minute diameter.

In a human cell, DNA is wound around proteins called histones, to make its length manageable by the cell. 170 to 240 base pairs of DNA are wound around 8 histone molecules to make an entity called a nucleosome. These nucleosomes are further condensed into a more compact and stable structure called the chromosome.

These chromosomes are so small that they fit into a cell organelle called the nucleus. DNA, in the form of chromosomes, cannot undergo central dogma and produce proteins; hence DNA is usually stored in the form of chromatin. During cell division, chromatin is condensed into chromosomes with the help of a protein called the condensin.

The connection between genes and alleles

Each chromosome pair carries the same set of genes. Even the location of these genes is identical in each chromosome. However, one chromosome in each pair is inherited from the father and the other from the mother. So, the person will have two copies of the same gene but the expression of each will be different. These two different copies that are inherited separately from each parent are called alleles.

An individual may have two different alleles of the same gene or the same allele for the gene. For example, while looking at the inheritance of eye color, a person might have two alleles that code for blue eyes or they might have one allele for blue eyes and the other for brown eyes depending on what they inherited from their parents. When both the alleles are the same, they are known as homozygous alleles whereas when the two alleles are different, they are known as heterozygous alleles.

Let's now talk about how a cell divides and how these genes are passed down from parent to progeny.

Mitosis

Mitosis is the process that defines how a cell divides to produce identical copies of itself as two daughter cells.

Firstly, each chromosome makes a copy of itself and each copy along with its original chromosome is referred to as a pair of sister chromatids. Then the nuclear membrane dissolves so that the chromatids can spread out into the rest of the cell. These chromatids align themselves in the center of the cell and the sister chromatids are pulled to opposite sides of the cell due to their polarity. After they separate, they are known as chromosomes again and each individual set is again enclosed in a new nuclear membrane. Then, the cell divides into half at the center with each set in two different halves. Each of these halves becomes a new cell that is identical to the original cell.

Mitosis is the step of cell division that is also found after fertilization. After the ovum is fertilized and becomes a zygote, it undergoes mitosis to form a mass of cells. It first divides to form two cells, then four, then eight, sixteen, thirty two cells and so on.

Meiosis

The process by which new cells with half the number of chromosomes are produced is known as meiosis. For example, humans are in a diploid state with a total of 46 chromosomes. Meiosis produces cells that have 23 chromosomes. This is state is known as the haploid state. Meiosis is seen during gamete formation.

The reason that meiosis is needed during gamete formation is that only when each gamete has had a haploid number of chromosomes will they be able to fuse during fertilization and give rise to a diploid zygote. Otherwise, if each gamete had 46 chromosomes, then the zygote would have double the chromosomes necessary for an individual, which would be a problem. The number of chromosomes would never be stable between two different generations.

There are two processes that occur in meiosis. The first is Meiosis I, which is a reduction process. This is followed by Meiosis II, which is division. Meiosis I is responsible of reducing a diploid cell to haploid while Meiosis II divides the haploid cell in a mitosis-like division. Each of the two processes has four phases that are: Prophase I, Metaphase I, Anaphase I and Telophase I for Meiosis I and Prophase II, Metaphase II, Anaphase II and Telophase II for Meiosis II.

Prophase I is involved in the pairing of the homologous chromosomes to form a tetrad. Each tetrad is composed of two sister chromatids. Crossing over occurs at this point during which the chromatids break down and rearrange themselves. At the end of Prophase I, the homologous chromosomes start to separate out but they still remain attached at the chiasmata. Chiasmata is the bridging structure between the chromosomes.

Metaphase I is the phase where the tetrads align along the center of the spindle. These spindle fibers attach to the centromere of each chromosome pair by special structures known as kinetochores. The opposing pull of the kinetochores creates a tension. The cells wait till the tension is gone and the chromosomes are properly oriented before they move over to anaphase.

Anaphase I is the part of meiosis where the tetrads separate and move to opposite poles. The centromeres remain intact in this phase.

Telophase I is when the two tetrads are separate from each other and form one set of chromosomes. Each chromosome set on opposite ends is completely separated and a nuclear membrane forms around them and the cells divide into two.

Prophase II is indicated by the dissolution of the nuclear envelopes that are formed in Telophase I. The spindle fibers are formed again. The chromatids thicken and shorten in this phase. The spindle fibers are arranged for the second meiotic division.

Metaphase II is characterized by the attachment of the centromeres to the spindle fibers from the centromeres is the opposite pole. The center plate is now at a 90° angle when compared to meiosis I.

Anaphase II follows metaphase II during which the centromeres are cleaved, allowing the sister chromatids to segregate. These chromatids are now known as chromosomes and move to opposite poles.

Meiosis ends with **Telophase II**, which is similar to Telophase I. The chromosomes decondense and lengthen in this phase. Nuclear envelopes form again and now four daughter cells are formed, each having a haploid set of chromosomes.

Chapter 3: An Overview of Inheritance

Inheritance or heredity is the concept of passing traits from parents to children. Traits are unique physical characteristics or qualities that are passed down through generations. Traits can be physical characteristics or behavioral characteristics or the predisposition to certain medical conditions.

Concept of Inheritance

Inheritance can be explained as a phenomenon through which traits or characters are passed on to the descendants from ancestors or the acquisition of traits genetically transmitted from parents to offspring would also be called inheritance.

The concept of inheritance was first given by an Austrian monk Gregor Mendel (1822- 1884). He extensively worked on the pea plant (Pisum sativum). He studied the flow of characteristics or traits from the parental generation to the offspring. He gave three laws, which are rules of thumb in any inheritance. His studies were neglected while he was alive, but were rediscovered after his death and he was given the title of "Father of Genetics."

Mendelian inheritance

Gregor Mendel studied inheritance characteristics in pea plants and proposed the famous Mendel's Laws of Inheritance. Mendel put in a lot of hard work and observation to reach the conclusions that he outlined in his laws.

Mendel chose pea plants because he could easily control their fertilization and growth. He tried two types of fertilization, self-fertilization and cross-fertilization. First, Mendel took pea plants and self-fertilized them. He observed the pea plants and their offspring for various generations. He observed that the traits of the parent generation were passed down intact to the progeny or F1 generation and all the following generations. He checked the self-fertilization inheritance over seven different traits: height (dwarf or tall), seed shape (wrinkled or smooth), pod shape (inflated or constricted), pod color (green or yellow), flower color (white or purple), flower position (axel or terminal) and seed color (yellow or green).

Mendel then conducted cross-pollination or cross-fertilization using purebred pea lines. Purebred pea plants are those that have undergone continuous self-pollination for several generations. Mendel chose 7 pairs of such pea plants with each pair containing one set of contrasting traits. For example, in a pair, one would have the trait of dwarfness while the other would have the trait of tallness. Similarly, each pair was characteristic for one trait that he wanted to test out of the seven mentioned previously.

Let us consider the example of tall versus dwarf plant. Mendel took a true breeding tall plant and cross-pollinated it with a true breeding dwarf plant. These were considered to be the parent generation. He then collected the seeds and grew them. These plants were considered to be the first filial generation or F1. It was observed that all the F1 plants were all tall. This observation was noted when he checked the other characteristics too. All the F1 progeny corresponded to one of the parents and not the other. Mendel then self-fertilized the F1 plants and grew the seeds. These plants were called the F2 generation. In the F2 generation, Mendel was surprised to see that some of the F2 generation plants were dwarf while others were tall. He was surprised that a trait not expressed in the F1 generation was seen in the F2 generation. The proportion of dwarf plants was found to be 1/4th of the total number of F2 plants while the remaining plants were tall. The tall and dwarf traits were identical to what was observed in the parent generation and no morphing or intermediate height was observed. Similar observations were made for the remaining six traits as well. He concluded that one trait was in F1 generation while in F2 generation both traits were seen in a proportion of 3:1 with the trait seen in F1 more prominent.

Using these observations, Mendel proposed that "factors" were being passed down from parent to offspring. These "factors" are now known to be genes. These genes are considered to be the units of inheritance. Genes consist of a pair of contrasting traits called alleles.

Mendel proposed that the trait observed in the F1 progeny is a dominant trait, which is why it is expressed in the majority of progeny. The dominant allele is denoted by a capital letter (T in the case of tall). The other trait is known as the recessive and is denoted by a small letter (t in the case of dwarf). Mendel proposed that the dominant trait would always be expressed if found even in only one allele while the recessive trait needed to be found in both alleles to be expressed.

Hence when we consider the above cross-pollination, we get

Parents   TT   tt

                  (Tall)   (Dwarf)

F1   Tt

                   (Tall)

(By self-pollinatio

F2   TT   Tt   Tt   tt

           (Tall) (Tall) (Tall) (Dwarf)

Hence in F2, the phenotypic ratio is Tall: dwarf is 3:1 while the genotypic ratio of TT:Tt:tt in 1:2:1.

The alleles, tt and TT are considered to be identical or homozygous while Tt is heterozygous. The alleles are known as genotypes while the descriptive terms of tall and dwarf are called phenotypes.

This kind of cross that has been explained is known as a monohybrid cross since only one pair of contrasting characteristics have been taken into consideration. In this cross, we can infer that the alleles are segregated randomly with a 50% chance of the progeny getting either of the alleles. From the physical appearance of the plant, one cannot determine whether the plant has the alleles TT or Tt. So Mendel proposed a test cross. In a test cross, a plant from the F2 was crossed with a recessive plant (dwarf plant). The progenies can easily be analyzed and the genotype of the F2 can be figured out. If the F2 was TT, then the test cross progeny will show only tall plants. However, if the F2 was Tt then the progeny of the test cross would show both tall and dwarf plants.

Similar to the monohybrid cross, Mendel tested out a dihybrid cross with two contrasting traits. He crossed a pea plant that had yellow colored seeds and round shape with one that had green colored seeds and wrinkled shape. Mendel found that the seeds from the parents were all yellow and round shaped. Yellow was dominant over green and round was dominant over wrinkled. He got the exact same results when he tried separate monohybrid crosses for the individual's traits. Hence the dominance of the individual traits was maintained even in a dihybrid cross without any interference from the other trait. Mendel found that when he self-pollinated the F1 generation plants, the F2 generation plants followed the same ratio of monohybrid cross. $3/4^{th}$ of the plants were yellow while $1/4^{th}$ of the plants were green. Similarly, the ratio of round to wrinkled seed shape was also 3:1.

Mendel's laws of inheritance
Law of segregation: -

The Law of Segregation states that every individual contains a pair of alleles (variants of the same character like blue and black color of the pupil) each of this trait or character segregates or separates during cell division and a randomly selected allele is passed on to the offspring. However, a homozygous parent produces gametes all of which have the same allele while a heterozygous parent produces two types of gametes each having a different type of allele. It is based on the fact that both the alleles do not mix and both are observed separately in the F2 generation even though one of them is missing in the F1.

Law of independent assortment:

The Law of Independent Assortment, also known as the "Inheritance Law," states that separate genes (genes are the part of DNA that make proteins or also called the expressed part of the DNA) separate traits or characteristics are passed independently of one another from parents to offspring irrespective of other traits.

Law of Dominance:

Mendel's law of dominance states that:

- ✓ Characters are controlled by units called "factors".
- ✓ These "factors" occur in pairs or alleles.
- ✓ If the person has a recessive allele and dominant allele, dominant allele will always mask up the recessive one.
- ✓ It also explains that only one of the parental alleles (dominant allele) is expressed in the F1 generation

whereas both the dominant and recessive are expressed in F2 generation.

These three laws of inheritance help us to study inheritance patterns in individuals. A summary can be drawn from all the three laws that alleles are passed on from parents to offspring, independent of other alleles; always the dominant allele overpowers the recessive allele and expresses itself.

Non-Mendelian Inheritance

Non-Mendelian is used to refer to any inheritance concepts that are not related to Mendel's laws. According to Mendelian inheritance, each parent plays a role in the traits received by their progeny. Mendel's laws come into effect when the genotype of the parents is known. There are several instances where the phenotypes observed in the offspring do not match the results predicted by Mendel's laws. These situations are explained using non-Mendelian inheritance.

Mendelian genetics doesn't take into account the possibility that other genes could influence the single gene that is being studied. This phenomenon of one gene influencing another is known as gene interaction. There are two types of gene interaction: intergenic and intragenic interactions.

Intergenic interactions are also known as non-allelic interactions. They occur between alleles on different genes that are located close together either on the same chromosome or different chromosomes. They cause a change in phenotypic expression. Supplementary genes, epistasis and lethal genes are some examples of intergenic interactions.

Intragenic interactions are inter-allelic interactions. These interactions occur between alleles on the same gene. Such interactions lead to the formation of phenotypes that are different from the usual dominant/recessive trait. Incomplete dominance and co-dominance are examples of such interactions.

The first concept is that of **Incomplete dominance.** When Mendel repeated his experiments using traits in other plants, he found some disparities. When he performed the experiments on Snapdragon, he found that the F1 generation had a phenotype that was not observed in either parent. For example, the flower color of the two parent Snapdragons was red (RR) and white (rr). However, the F1 progeny showed an intermediate color of pink. When these F1 progeny were further self pollinated, the F2 progeny followed the Mendelian genotypic ratio of 1 Red: 2 Pink: 1 White. However, the phenotypic ratio had changed from 3:1 to 1:2:1. It was found that the Red allele (R) was not completely dominant over the White allele (r) hence the Pink color (Rr). This was against the Law of Dominance. This kind of phenomenon was termed as incomplete dominance.

The next concept is **Co-dominance**. In the case of blood grouping, the alleles are expressed together with both alleles being equally dominant. This is a perfect example of co-dominance. Blood groups have three alleles: IA, IB and I. IA and IB produce different antigens while I doesn't produce any antigen. IA and IB are dominant over I but are equally dominant between each other. If a person has the alleles, IA and i, only the IA antigen is expressed on the surface of RBCs in the form of a sugar. Similarly, when IB and I are the two alleles IB gets expressed. However, if both IA and IB are found in a person, then they are both expressed and the person has the blood group AB. Hence, both IA and IB are expressed at the same level and are a perfect example of co-dominance. This is why there are four blood groups (A, B, O and AB) that are possible even though there are only three alleles. Blood grouping is also an example of **multiple alleles.**

There are six major types of non-Mendelian inheritance.

Extra nuclear inheritance

Extranuclear inheritance is also known as cytoplasmic inheritance that was first discovered in 1908 by Carl Correns. When Correns was working with the Four o'clock flower or *Mirabilis Jalapa*, he observed that the leaf color was entirely dependent on the maternal parent plant. When he focused his study on this aspect, he found that the trait was connected to a substance present in the cytoplasm of the ovule. Research by other scientists showed that it was DNA found in the chloroplasts that was responsible for the variation in inheritance. Further research also showed that DNA in the mitochondria also affected the inheritance pattern.

Endosymbiont theory is based on the idea that chloroplasts and mitochondria were once upon a time free organisms. Over time, these organelles formed a symbiotic relationship with the eukaryotic hosts in which they reside. It is the transfer of DNA of this DNA that is responsible for extranuclear inheritance. Since both chloroplast and mitochondria are present in the cytoplasm of maternal gametes only, the inheritance is passed down only through the maternal parent. Paternal gametes do not have cytoplasmic mitochondria and hence don't play a role in this inheritance.

In humans, diseases caused by this inheritance are known as mitochondrial diseases and are known to affect the eye and muscles.

Gene Conversion

Gene conversion is a compensation process in DNA recombination. In this form, a piece of DNA information is transferred from one DNA double helix to another. The first helix remains unaltered while the second helix gets altered. This phenomenon can occur as a mismatch repair between the two strands. Thus, it can convert one allele into another by transfer of information. It is frequently observed in fungi.

Infectious heredity

Infectious heredity is yet another type of non-Mendelian inheritance. Infectious organisms such as viruses infect the host cells and continue to live in the cytoplasm of these host cells. The presence of these viruses often leads to an altered phenotype of existing genes in the host cell. The progeny will inherit these altered phenotypes.

Since this phenotype is dependent on the virus or other infecting agents, the inheritance of the altered phenotype will be determined by the infectious state of the maternal parent. This results in uniparental inheritance that is similar to extranuclear inheritance.

An important and extensively studied example of this type of inheritance is that of yeast. 2 double-stranded RNA viruses, L and M, lead to this killer phenomenon exhibited by yeast. The L virus helps in the development of the capsid proteins for both viruses and also codes for RNA polymerase. Since the L virus is the one that produces RNA polymerase, which is required for replication, the M virus can only infect cells that are also infected by the L virus. The M virus code is for a toxin, which is produced from the host cell. This toxin kills all the susceptible cells that are in close proximity to the infected host cell. The M virus also makes the host immune to the toxic effect of the toxin. Susceptible cells are those that have only the L virus and lack the M virus.

The L and M viruses can only shift from one cell to another when their host cell is mating. Hence, they can only be transferred to the progeny. They will be passed down to every progeny.

Such traits that have been inherited by infection with foreign organisms or particles have also been observed in Drosophila or the fruit fly. The wild type flies recover after exposure to carbon dioxide. However, certain lines of these flies have shown extreme sensitivity to carbon dioxide. This sensitivity is found to have been inherited from mothers due to infection with a sigma virus that is capable of infecting only Drosophila.

While this type of inheritance is usually associated with virus, recent studies showed that certain bacteria is also capable of this type of infection followed by inheritance.

Genomic imprinting

Genes for a particular trait are passed down from parents to progeny. This is what traditionally happens in inheritance. In genomic imprinting, these genes are epigenetically marked, which means their level of expression gets altered. These markings are referred to as imprints. These imprints are formed before formation of gametes and are removed during the creation of germ line cells. Hence, a new imprint pattern is made with each generation.

The imprinting of genes depends on the origin of the chromosome that contains the said genes. In mice, the gene for insulin-like growth factor 2 undergoes genetic imprinting. The protein that is encoded by this gene helps in regulation of body size. Mice produce two functional copies that are larger in size than the two mutant copies. The size of the mice depends on the parent from which the wild allele is inherited. If the functional allele is inherited from the mother, then the baby mice will show dwarfism. If the functional allele is from the father, then the mice will be of normal size. This is because the maternal gene is imprinted which results in the inactivation of the gene that is inherited from the mother.

Imprints are formed as a result of methylation difference of the maternal and paternal alleles. This methylation leads to difference in expression between the two alleles from the two parents. Regions of significant methylation are connected to lower levels of gene expression. Unmethylated regions have a higher gene expression level. In this type of inheritance, the phenotype of the progeny is determined not only by allele transmitted but also by the sex of the parent from which the progeny has inherited the allele.

Mosaicism

Mosaics are people who possess cells that differ from other cells in their body due to genetic differences. These variations are due to mutations that occur in those specific cells or tissues at different levels of growth. Somatic mutations are those that happen in the non-gamete forming cells or tissues. Germline mutations are those that occur in the sperm or egg cells and will be passed on to the progeny. Mutations that are formed early on in growth will affect a much larger number of cells and hence only phenotypic expression can be used to identify such a person as a mosaic.

X-activation is a phenomenon that results in mutation. All female mammals possess two X chromosomes. To prevent lethal gene dosage, nature inactivates one of these X chromosomes after fertilization. This inactivation occurs randomly in all the cells in the body. Each X chromosome in a female has a different pattern of alleles because of which there will be different phenotypic expression in a cell depending on which chromosome is inactivated. Calico cats are the most commonly observed organisms that demonstrate this type of inheritance.

Trinucleotide repeat disorders

These are another type of non-Mendelian inheritance. They are caused due to an expansion of the microsatellite repeats that consist of 3 nucleotides. In normal people, the number of these tandem repeats is low. However, with each progressing generation there is a chance that the number of repeats could increase. When this occurs, the progeny can advance towards premutation. People with a large number of repeats that fall in the premutation range have an increased chance of having affected progeny. Those people who develop into the affected status will start exhibiting symptoms of their particular disease. Huntington's disease and Fragile X syndrome are two popular examples of this type of inheritance. Increased methylation and reduced expression of the fragile X mental retardation gene lead to the expression of the symptoms in the case of Fragile X syndrome.

Chapter 4: A Look at the Relation Between DNA and Inheritance

Since the previous chapter was totally about DNA, now recall its structure and function and imagine a molecule of DNA in your mind. As discussed earlier, it is a double helix molecule that is made up of monomers called nucleotides. It undergoes a process called the central dogma to produce proteins and proteins perform all the functions of our body. The function of DNA is not only making proteins that perform all functions of our body, but it also determines all our physical appearance and mental states like anger, memory and all others.

Have you ever wondered why some of us look like our parents? This is because our parents pass on their DNA to us and hence all their characteristics. This process is offspring acquiring DNA from their parents or ancestors is called inheritance.

Now the question arises "how did we get to know that DNA is our genetic material and responsible for inheritance?" There were a set of experiments conducted to prove this and the most famous among them is the "Hershey and Chase experiment."

The Hershey and Chase experiment

This experiment was conducted by Alfred Hershey and Martha Chase to determine the genetic material.

Hershey and Chase used bacteriophage (a virus that infects only bacteria). The structure of this virus was revealed using electron microscopy. The bacteriophage is made up of only two macromolecules proteins and DNA. Proteins gave it shape and DNA is its genetic material. The bacteriophage infects the host (bacterium) by attaching itself to its outer membrane. Then in injecting its genetic material (DNA) into the bacterium, leaves its empty protein coat attached to the bacterial outer membrane.

In their first attempt, Hershey and Chase experimented by labeling the DNA of Phages with radioactive species of Phosphorus that is P_{32} (they chose radioactive phosphorus because phosphorus is present only in DNA but not in any of the 20 amino acids that eventually make proteins). They allowed the bacteriophages to infect a bacterium species called E. coli, and through several refined experiments, they observed that the radioactive phosphorus species (P_{32}) was found in the cytoplasm of the bacterium.

They also conducted their experiments with a second marker that is radioactive sulfur S_{35} (this was based on the observation that sulfur is present only in sulfur containing amino acids like cysteine and methionine, but not present in DNA). They allowed these bacteriophages to infect E. coli.

They used a high-speed blender to remove the protein coat from the outer membrane of the bacterium; they centrifuged the blended suspension to separate protein coat and bacterium. Here they were able to find that the radioactive S35 present in the coat was not found inside the cytoplasm.

This experiment gave us a conclusion that DNA is the genetic material.

What do we get from our parents?

Humans are haploid (this means that we have two copies of the same chromosome); we have 23 pairs of chromosomes, from which 23 are from our father and 23 from our mother. Hence, an offspring is a combination of both mother and father. If it were to be so, we would have been half boy and half girl, which we are not. This is because though we have chromosomes from both our parents, only one of the set gets expressed at random.

Example: - We have 23 pairs of chromosomes namely pair 1, pair 2, pair 3 ... pair 23 (each pair consists of one chromosome from mom and one from dad). But only one chromosome among each pair is expressed to make your character. For an example from the first pair of chromosomes, we might be using chromosome that we have inherited from the mother and from the second pair we might be using a chromosome that we have inherited from our father.

This is the reason why our eye color might resemble our mother's eye color and we are blond like our father. Not only do we acquire their eye and hair colors, but we also acquire their strengths and weaknesses like immunity to cold or some other diseases and susceptibility to certain cancers.

Note: - The first 22 pairs of chromosomes are called autosomes, which determine all the characteristics of our body except sex. The last pair - that is the 23rd pair - is called the sex chromosome, which determines the sex. This is why some of us are boys and some are girls. In technical terms girls have XX in their 23rd pair of chromosomes and boys have XY in their 23rd pair.

How do we get one chromosome from Mom and one from Dad?

Have you ever wondered that how does a human body replenish cells in the place of an injury, where some of the cells are damaged? This is accomplished by a process called cell division. In cell division, a healthy and mature cell divides into two cells.

Cell division is different in different cells. In somatic or vegetative cells (like skin, endothelial cells and etc.), one cell divides into two daughter cells with the same number of chromosomes - that is 23 pairs. This process is called mitosis. In germ cells or reproductive cells (like sperm and ovum that are involved in sexual reproduction) one parent cell divides into four daughter cells with each daughter cell having half the number of chromosomes as the parent cell.

Outline of meiosis: - meiosis can be explained as the cell division in which the parent cell divides twice and hence produces four daughter cells that have half the number of chromosomes as the parent cell. It is a combination of reduction and division. Meiosis is instrumental in maintaining the diploid nature of a zygote.

When a sperm cell and an ovum (each having 23 chromosomes) fuse together they produce a cell called zygote that has 23 pairs of chromosomes - one from each parent. Zygote develops into an embryo. The embryo undergoes differentiation and produces a fetus (an unborn offspring of a mammal). This is how we get one chromosome from our mom and one from dad.

Impact of parental chromosomes on offspring

As discussed earlier, DNA is our genetic material and it makes what we are. As we inherit chromosomes from our parents, we inherit their appearance, intelligence, memory, resistance or susceptibility to diseases and even some genetic disorders.

Traits and heredity play an important role in the impact of chromosomes from parents to offspring. A child can inherit a physical trait such as hair type from either of the parents or could inherit a combination of the two parental traits to form a different hair type. Similarly, behavioral aspects are also inherited from the parents.

It is always observed that parents give birth to a baby who has a very rare and deadly genetic disorder, even though parents are perfectly healthy. The simple reason is that those parents might have inherited the gene for that disease from their parents or parents of their parents.

In early times, it was said that one could be a biological parent of their child, but anyone from the whole family could be their child's soul parent. The term "soul parent" was used to describe the person from the family that the child appears to have inherited his behavioral traits from.

With the advancement of life sciences, it was found that if same genes are expressed in two individuals of the family, they might have a characteristic in common. This characteristic can be anything from eye color to a deadly cancer.

This leaves us with a probability that healthy parents may give birth to an unhealthy child or blonde parents may give birth to a child whose hair is black. This seemed interesting to many scientists, anthropologists and historians, so they developed a branch of science called Genealogy. Genealogy is a science of studying ancestors and their descendants based on various factors like genetic analysis, family name, occupation and many more attributes.

The relationship between DNA and inheritance is clearly seen in humans not only in the form of physical appearance but also in the form of blood groups and certain physical characteristics.

Blood grouping

As we all know, while blood is made up of the same basic components, not all blood is the same. There are 8 blood types that are grouped based on the presence of certain antigens. Antigens are organic substances that have the capability of triggering a defense mechanism if they are foreign to the body. This is why blood typing is so important before blood transfusions or organ transplants.

Firstly, we have the **ABO blood grouping**. This grouping divides blood into for major group depending on the presence or absence of two specific antigens A and B. These two antigens are found on the surface of red blood cells (also denoted as RBCs), which make up the major part of the blood.

Blood Group A – This blood group is signified by the presence of only the A antigen on the RBCs.

Blood Group B – People with this blood group have only the B antigen on the surface of their RBCs.

Blood Group O – This blood group is given this name because it has neither the A antigen nor the B antigen.

Blood Group AB – People with this blood group have both the A and the B antigen on their RBCs.

The A and B antigens are dominant. Hence, a person can have the blood group A if they have both alleles that code for the A antigen or if one allele codes for A antigen and the other for no antigen. Since A is dominant over the lack of the antigen, only the A antigen gets expressed. If a person has both alleles that do not code for either antigen, then they are considered to be part of Blood Group O. Now, the unique thing is what if a person has both A and B alleles? What happens then? Do they fight it out? No. Each allele is represented equally and both A and B antigen get expressed. Such people belong to the Blood Group AB. Such a phenomenon is called co-dominance.

Each of the above blood groups is further divided into two depending upon the **Rh factor.** Rh factor is another antigen that is present on the RBCs. Rh factor stands for the Rhesus factor since it was first discovered in Rhesus monkeys.

Each blood group is further labeled positive (+) or negative (-) depending on the presence or absence of this Rh factor.

So now we have 8 blood types: A+, A-, B+, B-, O+, O-, AB+ and AB-.

A person inherits one of these blood groups because of genes that he inherited from his parents, which decide which of the

8 groups he belongs to. As you know, each gene has two alleles and the characteristic shown by the child is decided by which of the two are inherited from each parent.

Consider a situation wherein, the mother is A+ with one A allele and one O allele with one being Rh+ and the Rh- and the father has O+ with both O alleles and one Rh+ while the other is Rh-. Then according to Mendelian laws, the child can either be:
1) AO with Rh+ and Rh- or
2) AO with both Rh+ or
3) AO with both Rh - or
4) OO with Rh+ and Rh- or
5) OO with both Rh+ or
6) OO with both Rh-.

In the cases 1) and 2), the child will have a blood group, A+ because both A and Rh+ are dominant. In 3), the progeny will be A- because both the recessive Rh- alleles are inherited from the parents. In 4) and 5), the child will be O+ because both the recessive O alleles have been inherited. In 6), the child will be O- because both the alleles for each antigen that are inherited are the recessive O and Rh-.

Hence, even our blood comes from parents. This is why for blood transfusions or organ transplants, parents or siblings or children are considered first before seeking other possible donors. The chances of their blood type matching the patient's are more likely.

Dimples

Dimples are natural marks or depressions on the cheeks. They can be either on one cheek or on both cheeks. Some people are born with dimples while others develop dimples as they age. People born with dimples can also lose their dimples after an age.

Anatomically speaking, dimples are considered to be formed due to differences in the facial muscles known as the zygomaticus major. When these muscles are shortened they pull at the skin causing dimples to form.

Dimples are considered to be caused by a single gene that is inherited from parents. Dimples were initially considered to be dominant traits. Parents who had dimples were sure to give birth to a baby with dimples. If one of the parents has dimples, the child had a 25% or 50% chance of inheriting the gene for dimples. However, after extensive studies it was found that dimples are not always dominant traits. Hence it was labeled as an "irregular" dominant trait. It was also proposed that the ability to have dimples could be controlled by more than one single gene.

However, dimples can also be caused by spontaneous mutation. Such dimples are usually seen on one side of the cheeks rather than both. They can also be seen on the chin. Such dimples are not inherited from parents and are a freak mutation that leads to the formation of an indentation on the skin.

Handedness

As you would have observed, most of the world is right handed. Many feel that the proclivity for some people to use their right hand over their left or vice versa is more due to their environment than genes. However, this isn't entirely true. While there are indications that handedness is influenced by the environment the child grows up in, it is also seen that genes do play a role in defining whether a child is right handed or left handed. It is believed that there are various genes that play a role in the handedness of a child. Most of these genes are connected to brain function and activity, mainly in the left side of the brain.

The trait for right or left-handedness doesn't follow the simple dominant or recessive inheritance pattern. It is influenced by many genes and the environment. It was initially believed by Charles Darwin that the gene that influences handedness was passed down much like any other trait. However, later on, people disproved this and came up with the conclusion that this trait is influenced both by genes and environment. There was also the cultural stigma against being left handed to be considered. Many cultures feel that left-handedness is something wrong and constantly make their child use their right hand, thereby ensuring that the dominant hand becomes the right hand even it is the child is left handed by birth.

The most popular genetic model for this trait is the Right Shift Theory. This theory was developed in 1972 by Marian Annett, a British psychologist. According to this theory, consider a hypothetical RS+ gene that is involved in the development of the speech processing units and the motor cortex of the left side of the brain. The contrasting allele of this gene is the RS-, which rather than cause left-handedness just has no preference for either. It is indifferent to the direction of motor activity. This theory suggests that the genes are co-dominant rather than the usual dominant or recessive type.

Hence, left-handers inherit a lack of hand preference rather than inherit a gene that makes them left-handed. They lack a neurological impulse to use the right hand instead of the left hand. Therefore, this gene just ensures that people with this gene prefer their right hand to their left while those with the negative allele have no specific preference and hence can be either right handed or left handed. Since there are two alleles, there are a total of three possible combinations that can arise: RS+RS+, RS+RS- or RS-RS-. Therefore, majority of people have at least one allele of RS+, which makes them prone to increased strength in the left hemisphere, which leads to right-handedness. Those with the double recessive alleles could be either right handed or left handed or maybe even ambidextrous. In those people lacking the RS+ gene, the environment in which they are brought up could eventually decide whether they are right handed or left handed. Hence, the genes make a difference only to right-handers and not to the left-handers.

This theory takes everything into consideration. It even explains how identical twins can have different hand preferences. Marian Annett perfected this theory over time, and proposed that the existence of the RS- gene counter-balances the RS+ gene which is more dominant that the RS- gene. This refined theory was called the Balanced Polymorphism Theory.

Another similar theory was proposed by Chris McManus. He proposed that there exist two alleles of a gene that control the handedness of a person. One is the dextral (D) allele, which is inclined towards right-handedness while the other is the chance (C) allele, which is neutral. According to this, the DD genotype gives rise to only right-handers, while the CC gives rise to either right-handers or left-handers equally. The DC genotype gives rise to 25% left-handers and 75% right-handers.

On the whole, no genetic proof has been found for either of the above two theories. While scientists at Oxford have come quite close to finding the genes for handedness, there is no concrete proof either proving or disproving both the theories. With wonders happening in the field of genetic mapping, it might not be too long before someone discovers the genes responsible not only for handedness but for a dozen other characteristics that haven't been explained yet.

Freckles

Freckles are small spots usually seen on people with fair skin. Freckles contain a pigment called melanin. Melanin is formed when harmful UV rays hit our skin. Melanin protects our skin from these harmful rays. Special cells in the skin called melanocytes produce these melanin pigments. In some people, they melanocytes are spread out over their skin and this is why some people tan easily. Others, however, have melanocytes in clumps all over their skin and hence end up with clumps of melanin. These clumps are known as freckles.

People observed that there was a connection between red hair and freckles. They noticed that all red-haired people had freckles. It was later discovered that this was because both red hair and freckles are controlled by the same gene, MC1R.

MC1R protein is found on the outer membrane of melanocytes. This protein helps in making sure that there is a balance of pigments in the skin and hair. There is a pigment called pheomelanin that is responsible for red hair and the reddish color of freckles. Mc1R converts all of this pigment into eumelanin. Hence when there is a mutation in MC1R gene, it leads to red hair and freckles. If one allele of the gene doesn't work, people get only freckles. However, if both copies are defective then it leads to both red hair as well as freckles.

People with any hair color other than red get freckles due to a buildup of MC1R gene. Scientists aren't sure exactly how the gene codes for the formation of freckles. Scientists in China recently found a gene on the chromosome 4 that also causes freckles. This leads to the possibility that there are many genes that help in the formation of freckles and we have just discovered two of them.

Curly hair

Hair, as we all know, is made of keratin, which forms a stable filament. This filament makes the hair strong. The hair grows inside the skin in a cavity called the follicle. This follicle is the only living part of the hair. Hair consists of three parts: the cuticle, cortex and the medulla. The shape of the fiber and the cortex is what decides the straightness or curliness of hair. Round fibers result in straight hair while c-shaped follicles form curly hair and oval fibers form wavy hair.

Hair texture is controlled by genes that are incompletely dominant. This means that they can code for straight, curly or any form in-between the two. Let us consider two versions of the hair type gene. One is the curly gene (C) and the other is the straight gene (s). Between these two genes, there is no completely dominant gene. When the genotype of the child is CC, then he or she will have curly hair and when the child has the ss genes, he or she will have straight hair. Now what about the genotype Cs? Will the child have curly hair since it is denoted as the dominant? This is where the concept of incomplete dominance comes into play. According to this concept, in the event of a child having the genotype Cs, the child will have neither curly nor straight hair. Instead the child will have wavy hair.

The gene responsible for forming curls was identified as the trichohyalin gene. This gene has been known to play a role in the development of follicles. However, it was only recently found to play a role in curliness as well. Scientists believe that a variation in this gene determines the curliness or straightness of hair. Studies also showed that curly hair is, even though incompletely dominant, still dominant over straight hair.

However, studies also showed that there are variations in the hair type genes from continent to continent. For example, curly hair is rare in Asians while it is very common amongst Africans. It is believed that various other genes also control hair type in different populations and sometimes there are genes that are unique to a particular population that are not seen in other people from other continents.

Red/Green color-blindness
Red/green colorblindness is an example of recessive x-linked inheritance. This means that the gene causing this trait is located on the X chromosome. Hence, the female members in a family usually carry this trait. However, it can be expressed in both the male and female progeny depending on the genotype of the parents. The males are more likely to exhibit this trait since they have just one X chromosome, which means they have a 50% chance of being colorblind. Women, on the other hand, need both X chromosomes to be recessive for the trait to be expressed. Since women have two

X chromosomes and this trait is a recessive trait, they would need both the recessive alleles to be colorblind. If they have just one copy, then they are just carriers. They could possibly transfer the trait to their progeny.

A single gene located on the X chromosome causes colorblindness. People who express this gene cannot differentiate between red and green. Let X^C denote the recessive allele and X^+ denote the dominant allele. Now the recessive, X^c, causes colorblindness. Consider a female who has the genotype X^cX^+ and a man who has the genotype X^+Y. Their progeny could by X^cX+ or X^cY or X^+X^+ or X^+Y. This means they could have a son who is colorblind but their other three children (two daughters and one other son) will not express the trait. However, one daughter will be a carrier.

If the father was also colorblind, then their progeny would be the following: one colorblind daughter, one daughter who is a carrier, one colorblind son and one son who is neither a carrier nor is he infected.

Similarly, if the mother was colorblind and the father wasn't, then the progeny would be: two carrier daughters and two sons both of whom would be colorblind.

Only if both parents are colorblind will all the children be colorblind.

Hairline shape

If a person's hairline forms a peak at the center of the forehead, they are said to have a widow's peak. People who don't have this point are considered to have a straight hairline. Widow's peak is considered to be a dominant trait.

The inheritance of this shape is very simple. It follows the law of dominance and is not complicated.

When a trait is considered to be dominant, it means that even a single allele is enough for the trait to be expressed. This dominant allele will overshadow the recessive allele. In the case of hairline shape, let W denote the dominant allele that causes the widow's peak and w represent the recessive allele. Now, a person with either WW or Ww will have a widow's peak because of the presence of at least one allele of the dominant allele (W). Only those with the genotype ww will have a straight hairline.

In the case of inheritance, the genotype of the parents matters. If one parent is homozygous dominant (WW) and the other recessive (ww), then the progeny will be heterozygous (Ww) which means that they will all have a widow's peak. If both parents are heterozygous, then $3/4^{th}$ of the progeny will have a widow's peak while the remaining will have a straight hairline.

If one parent is homozygous dominant (WW) and the other heterozygous (Ww), then all the progeny will have a widow's peak. If one parent is homozygous recessive (ww) and the other heterozygous (Ww), then 50% of the offspring will have a widow's peak while the other half will have a straight hairline.

PTC tasting

Phenylthiocarbamide (PTC) is a chemical that mimics the taste of some vegetables such as broccoli and also certain poisonous plant compounds. While humans normally don't ingest PTC, they ingest derivatives of this chemical found in vegetables such as cabbage and broccoli.

The curious thing about this chemical and its derivatives is that their taste seems to depend on the genetic makeup of the person ingesting it. To about 75% of the human population, this chemical tastes bitter and to the remaining it has no taste.

Arthur Fox first observed this variation in taste when he accidentally blew some powdered PTC into the air and his colleague remarked on the horribly bitter taste of the dust. However, Fox couldn't taste a thing. Fox then made all his friends and family taste it and found that they all exhibited different reactions to it. Some couldn't taste a thing while others found it extremely bitter. A select few even found it to be mildly bitter.

Soon after this, it was determined that genes play a major role in the tasting of PTC. Initially, the gene for PTC was considered to be a dominant trait. A dominant trait means that the trait will be expressed even if a single allele codes for the trait. A single copy of a dominant trait is more than enough for it to be expressed in an individual. As far as PTC tasting is concerned, the bitter taste is controlled by the dominant allele and the lack of taste is represented by the recessive allele.

The single gene for PTC tasting helps in coding for a taste receptor on our tongue. Of the two alleles, one is the tasting allele and the other is the non-tasting allele. Each of these allele codes for a receptor protein with a slight difference in shape. In 2003, the gene was identified as TAS2R38. It was soon found that instead of being dominant, the PTC gene is incompletely dominant. This was because some people had a mild reaction to this chemical. The levels of bitterness were varied between people, leading the scientists to believe that it was incompletely dominant. People with both alleles as dominant will taste extreme bitterness while those with both recessive will taste nothing. People with a heterozygous genotype will taste a slight bitter taste.

Polydactyly

Polydactyly is a condition where a person has an extra finger or toe. While this condition is genetic, it is not related to any other disease or disorder. It is caused by a mutation in chromosome 7 that is inherited from the previous generations. While it isn't rare in the population, it isn't very common either. The extra fingers or toes are usually underdeveloped and are just a mass of tissue. In some cases these extra digits are functional.

One of the genes that cause Polydactyly is GLI3, which is transcriptional repressor. It codes for a DNA-binding protein that regulates the expression of a number of genes. There are two types of Polydactyly that are caused by mutation in this gene.

The first type is known as **Pre-axial Polydactyly.** This is more common in Asian populations where the extra digit is either a thumb or the big toe. A popular example of a person who has this type of Polydactyly is the Bollywood actor Hrithik Roshan. The genetic model of this type is not well understood but congenital abnormalities are considered to go hand in hand with this type of Polydactyly. Mutation in the gene GLI3 purports to be partly responsible for this Polydactyly.

The next type of Polydactyly is known as an **Isolated post-axial Polydactyly**, which is more common in African-

Americans. People with this condition tend to have extra fingers or toes on the side of the small digit.

There are several subtypes of the above two types of Polydactyly which are divided based on the location, functionality and severity of the growth.

Surprisingly, Polydactyly is inherited as an autosomal dominant trait. This means that the gene for this trait is on one of the 22 autosomes and is not sex linked. It also means that a single dominant allele is enough for the trait to be expressed in a child. It is believed that Polydactyly is caused by a group of genes. The presence of one, some or all of these genes is enough for the trait to be expressed. If a child possesses the dominant allele of any of these genes, then they express the trait. There are various genes that are responsible for the digits on our hands or feet. Some may determine the position of the digit, some the size, and some the existence of the digit itself. When there is a problem with any of these genes, it could lead to Polydactyly.

Polydactyly can also be a result of other syndromes such as Cephalopolysyndactyly Syndrome (GCPS) or Trisomy 13.

Earlobe attachment

Earlobes are known to have two forms: the detached dominant form where the lobes are not attached to the side of the head and the attached recessive form where the lobes are connected to the side of the head. Earlobe inheritance is considered to be a continuous trait. It follows a method of incomplete dominance. This was seen by the fact that some people have neither purely detached nor attached lobes but a form in-between the two.

Detached lobes are considered to be the dominant trait over the attached lobes. It is also believed that there are many genes that contribute to the inheritance of this trait. Since the attachment also changes the shape of the ear, there might be many genes involved in this trait.

Consider that the allele for free earlobes is represented by the dominant G and the allele for the attached lobes is represented by the recessive g. So people with a homozygous GG genotype will have free or detached earlobes while people with homozygous recessive gg genotype will have attached earlobes. However, people with heterozygous Gg will not show the dominant trait; instead they will show a trait that is in-between the two.

Earwax

Earwax is also known as cerumen and is produced by glands along the lining of the ear canal. As more and more earwax is formed, it moves out of the ear carrying debris and dead cells with it. There are two types of earwax that a person can have. One is the dry, flaky, grayish earwax and the other is the gooey, stinky, yellow type.

Type of earwax is determined by variation at a single gene. The wet earwax is dominant over the dry, flaky earwax. Even though wet earwax is considered to be the dominant allele, it isn't very common in some parts of the world.

The gene responsible for the two types of earwax is believed to be a gene that alters the shape of the channel that controls the flow of molecules that affect the earwax form. Let us consider that the allele for the dominant wet earwax is W and the recessive dry earwax is w. So people with homozygous WW will have wet, yellow earwax while people with homozygous ww will have dry, flaky, grayish earwax. People with heterozygous Ww genotype also had wet, yellow earwax which clearly shows that wet is dominant over dry.

However, the percentage of people expressing the dominant trait varies from continent to continent with Asians expressing the recessive trait more than the dominant trait while Africans and Europeans express the dominant trait to almost a 100%.

Cleft chin

A cleft chin is a mark on the face that looks like a dimple on a person's chin. This condition is caused by a problem in the fusing of the lower jaw. When the lower half of the jaw fails to fuse properly during fetal development a cleft chin is formed. Cleft chin is an inherited trait.

While it is mostly seen in men, it isn't sex-linked. It is an autosomal dominant trait. Even though it is a dominant trait, the number of people with cleft chins is lesser than those with normal chins.

The allele for a cleft chin is a dominant allele that masks the recessive normal allele. The dominant allele is symbolized C and expresses the cleft chin trait while the recessive allele is symbolized by c and expresses a normal chin. For a person to have a cleft chin, he or she should have at least one dominant allele for the trait. If a person is homozygous dominant (CC) or heterozygous (Cc) he or she will have cleft chin. If a person is homozygous recessive (cc) then he or she would have a normal chin. Hence, parents who are homozygous dominant will for sure give rise to offspring that have a cleft chin. Heterozygous parents have a 1/4th chance of having a child who has a normal chin. If both parents are homozygous recessive, then all their children will have normal chins. If one parent is heterozygous and the other homozygous dominant, then the children will all have a cleft chin. If one parent is heterozygous and the other homozygous recessive, then the children will have a 50% chance of having a cleft chin.

Lactose intolerance

Lactose intolerance is when the ability to digest lactose goes awry. Lactose is a sugar found in dairy products. Lactose is broken down by lactase which is an enzyme produced by the cells in the small intestine lining.

Congenital lactase deficiency is a disorder by which infants are incapable of breaking down the lactose in breast milk or formula milk. Lactose intolerance could lead to severe diarrhea and dehydration and weight loss in infants. Infants need to be fed with lactose-free infant formula. Lactose intolerance in adults is because of decrease in the production of the enzyme lactase. People with lactose intolerance might experience severe abdominal pain, bloating, nausea and diarrhea when they consume dairy products. People who suffer from lactase nonpersistence have some lactase activity and can consume varying amounts of lactose in their daily diets without falling sick.

Lactose intolerance in infants is due to mutations in the LCT gene. LCT codes for the enzyme lactase. Mutations in this gene cause congenital lactase deficiency by interfering with the function of lactase.

While lactose intolerance in infants is caused by mutations in the LCT gene, for adults lactose intolerance is due to a decrease in activity of this LCT gene. The expression of this gene is controlled by a regulatory element, which is located in a neighboring gene called MCM6. Some individuals inherit changes or mutations to this regulatory element, which enable them to digest lactose throughout their lifetime. People who lack this change lose their ability to digest lactose as they age and hence become intolerant to lactose.

The lactose intolerant gene is a recessive trait. Two copies of the non-functional gene are required for the trait to get expressed. This gene (LCT) comes in two forms. One form enables us to keep up lactase production as we age while the other one stops as the person ages. To be lactose intolerant, a person must inherit both the recessive alleles from their parents. Since it is a recessive trait, only a homozygous recessive genotype will lead to lactose intolerance. A heterozygous and a homozygous dominant genotype lead to normal lactase production.

The lactase gene works the same way in everybody from when they are infants. But this gene is switched off when the child stops drinking mother's milk. Scientists propose that this gene has a repressor that lies on the lactase DNA. So later on in life, this repressor hides the gene and no lactase is made. Mutations could lead to this repressor being inactive which means that lactase is continuously produced. However, scientists aren't exactly sure how the in-depth mechanism of lactose intolerance switch works.

Hand clasping

Hand clasping is a trait where each finger of one hand is superimposed on the finger of the other hand. There are two ways in which people can superimpose their fingers. One way is to place the right fingers over the fingers from the left hand. People who follow this are part of the R (right) phenotype. The other type is the opposite with the left fingers over the right. This is known as the L (left) phenotype.

Most people have a specific preference as to which finger comes on the top. Once a person starts one of the methods they consistently follow the same habit throughout their life. Studies found that the R phenotype was more popular over the L phenotype in women while the opposite was observed in men.

When extensive studies were done to figure out the inheritance of these characters, it was found that the inheritance wasn't as simple as dominant or recessive traits of a gene. It is believed that there is more than one gene that is responsible for hand clasping and that it is also influenced by environmental factors. One study found that 45% of the population places their right thumb over the left hence becoming a part of the R phenotype while the L phenotype was more popular with 55% of the population following this phenotype.

Chapter 5: Everything You Need to Know About Genealogy

Genealogy means knowledge of generations (in Greek) It is also known as family history. It is the study of families and tracing of their lineages (the web of social relationships) and history. The person who studies Genealogy is called a genealogist. Generally, genealogists use interviews, historical records, genetic analysis and, sometimes even software to obtain information about a family to demonstrate to its members.

Why is Genealogy important?

"Genealogy is a curiosity for most, hobby for many, but an obsession for few."

People around us might have very specific reasons for tracing their family histories. Others research their family history without giving it much importance. Some do this research to gain more knowledge of their ancestors and to motivate their family members.

Genealogy obviously means different things to different people. Different people might expect different outcomes from this research. But some of the major reasons why people delve into Genealogy are:

- Most of the people want to validate stories told about their family and ancestors.
- To find out whether one is related to any famous person. This sometimes involves tracing the roots as far as distant ancestors and coming back to the present generation through a different branch.
- Gaining the knowledge of an ancestor's involvement in any famous historical event.
- The area of concern nowadays is medical history. Genealogy is most often used by genetic counselors to get the medical history of family members, which is used to predict the health of the fetus.
- To settle questions of property ownership by showing descent proof.
- Also used to find out the ancestor who one resembles.
- To find out biological parents of an adopted child and to find children who were given for adoption.
- Paternity proof.
- To find original religion of ancestors and the whole family.
- Preserving family tradition and passing it on to future generations.
- To glimpse ancestors' experiences and feelings.
- To find and reconnect with living relatives.
- The most important among all the reasons might be to make a family tree.

History of Genealogy

In many parts of the world, Genealogy was given different names but had the same level of importance.

Family descent was of utmost importance to the ancient Hebrews. Often Hebrew males had to prove themselves as the descendants of Aaron or as the brother of Moses, in order to hold the priesthood and importance in the society and community that prevailed in those times.

The ancient Greeks gave Genealogy as much importance as their neighbors, but their ultimate goal was to prove that they were descendants from a god or goddess. This was crucial in order to lead life with a good social status and respect in the community. Genealogy made a recognized place in Greek history from as early as 5th century but was very unscientific when compared to the modern standards put up by the research community.

It largely contained material from epic poetry. The two great poems, the Iliad and the Odyssey, were usually taken into consideration. It is always possible that the poet might have written about fictional characters. But archaeological studies and findings of the past 125 years have shown that most of the facts given in these two epic poems were true.

The ancient Assyrians also kept records of their ancestors and descendants, using a form of writing called cuneiform which was inscribed onto clay tablets. Over 20,000 such tablets were taken out in the palace library during archeological excavations in the 1840s.

The ancient Chinese had a succession of dynasties; they also documented names of the rulers and emperors carefully. The first to be documented was the Qin Dynasty that ruled a large part of China between 221-206 BC. The modern name of China comes from the ruler of the Qin Dynasty, Ch'in. The last Chinese dynasty was the Qing Dynasty that ruled from 1644 to 1911 and that also gave immense importance to Genealogy. Chinese religions promote active worship of ancestors. So descendants had to know the identity of their ancestors from this religious perspective. From these studies, it was found that Kung Fu and Shaolin originated in India and were taken to China by an Indian monk.

Genealogy also played a major role in Indian dynasties. Disagreement among brothers over power and rule lead to the famous battle of Mahabharata. Indian rulers, like all other rulers around the world, passed on the power to their descendants. So it was very crucial to document rulers and their children to avoid conflicts.

One among the interesting Genealogy goes back to the time of the Inca civilization. Here, people managed to have a genealogical record despite having no written language. Inca civilization lived along the western coast of South America near 5th century AD; the millions of Incas believed that their emperor 'Tawantinsuyu' was a descendant of the Sun God Viracocha. The emperor selected administrators from his sons and some extended kin (no women were given high posts). Only those who descended from the pure bloodline held important positions in the government, religion and the military.

In the history of the west, the role of Genealogy was to find out the descent and kinship of rulers and nobles, who often argued for the purpose of claiming wealth and power.

Modern Genealogy

Unlike in ancient Genealogy, modern Genealogy is not concerned about passing on the power of rule, but more concerned with claiming the property of ancestors.

Today Genealogy is more of a hobby and people are trying to find their ancestors for recreation purposes and knowledge of their past.

In the modern era, Genealogy has become more widespread. Genealogy received an appreciable boost in 1970 with the broadcast of Roots: The Saga of an American Family, Alex Haley's account of his family line on television. With the arrival of the Internet, the number of resources increased to genealogists, resulting in a blast of interest on the topic for research purposes. Some sources also say that Genealogy is one of the most popular topics being searched on the Internet.

Different sources of study and information

Genealogy uses different criteria for studying for studying people and their family history. A genealogist often relies on more than one sources of information to get accurate data. Genealogist may do genetic analysis, oral interviews and collect information from the Internet to study a person's family history.

These are some of the various sources of information that a genealogist might use to obtain an accurate history.

Genetic analysis: - This is one of the most precise and dependable sources of information. It is being used extensively by modern genealogists to find the relationship between people in the same family and people of different families as well. It can use mitochondrial DNA, ribosomal RNA, Y chromosome or autosomal DNA for this purpose. This is so precise that it can uncover relatives from any branch of the family.

Let's consider each of the four analyses mentioned above in detail.

Y chromosome

Y chromosome is characteristic of males. It is transferred directly from father to son. While women have XX sex chromosomes, men have XY chromosomes, which is why we can use this Y chromosome to go back and look for information that is transmitted along the male line. The testing is done to a particular location of the Y chromosome called the marker. This varies according to the part of the chromosome that is being tested. These markers are often sites for mutation to occur. When such a mutation occurs, it becomes unique to that person and to his male progeny until another mutation overthrows the existing one. These mutations could be harmless. They need not necessarily lead to a disease or physical change. However, using these mutations, a person's ancestry or family can be found. Each of these markers can either be a short tandem repeat (STR) or a single nucleotide polymorphism (SNP). STRs are so called because a short sequence of DNA repeats itself multiple times. STRs are often known as microsatellites and are the markers most commonly used in Y-chromosome testing. STRs occur at specific locations on the chromosome and hence are named depending on their location. When STRs are used the most recent ancestry of the patient can be predicted.

Another type of marker is based on mutation in a single base substitution. This is an SNP, which is comparatively rarer than an STR. Since these are so rare, it can be assumed that everyone who has a specific SNP is related. These form haplogroups and each haplogroup is usually defined by a single ancestry with a specific SNP. SNP is extremely useful in getting to know a person's ancient ancestry.

During Y testing, the STR marker results show the number of times that the body sequence repeats itself. This number is called allele value. The result at the end of a Y testing is called a haplotype. It contains a string of allele values. These results can be used to estimate the patient's haplogroup. While a haplogroup is useful for SNP rather than STR, haplogroups can also be formed for STR tests. To pinpoint the exact ancestry of a person, just an STR test or just a SNP test is not sufficient. Both are equally important for determining ancestry. From these tests, the major population to which the patient belongs to can be identified. For further in-depth understanding, a "backbone" haplogroup test can be done to confirm the basic haplogroup. A "deep clade" test identifies which specific branch of the haplogroup the patient belongs to. From this, the end result would give the person knowledge about both his ancient as well as recent ancestry.

There are a variety of applications for Y-DNA testing. Y-DNA testing can be used to check the genealogical research for your family tree. It can also determine which family trees with similar or the same surnames are related, and it can provide clues with genealogy research.

Mitochondrial DNA

Mitochondria are part almost every cell in the body. The main function of the mitochondria is to procure useful energy from food. It has to convert food into energy that can be used by the cell, which it does by a process known as oxidative phosphorylation. Mitochondria can also help in controlling apoptosis or cell death. They are also a part of hemoglobin and are essential in cholesterol production. While most of the cellular DNA is stored in the nucleus, mitochondria has its own genome and hence DNA. The mitochondrial DNA is circular and very similar to bacterial DNA.

Mitochondrial DNA is passed down from mother to child. Only females pass down this DNA so testing of this DNA in an individual will give details about their maternal line. Since both males and females have this DNA, it is easy to test. Mutations in this DNA, unlike the Y chromosome are slow. These mutations build up over centuries and hence a testing of mitochondrial DNA will enable us to identify the origin of a person's lineage. Each mutation will connect the mitochondrial DNA to a specific haplogroup. And this haplogroup will identify the person's ancient maternal lineage. After testing the mitochondrial DNA, it is compared to a reference called the Cambridge Reference Sequence (CRS). CRS is used to identify which specific haplotype the mitochondrial DNA belongs. People with the same haplotype share a common maternal ancestor somewhere in the past. The common ancestor could be as recent as a few generations or as far back as a few centuries. The DNA can then be connected to specific haplogroups. This identification will give us which ancient region or continent specific population the patient belongs to.

Autosomal DNA

We have discussed about finding the maternal and paternal ancestry of a person through the mitochondrial DNA and Y chromosome respectively. Now we will talk about autosomal DNA.

Let's start at the basics first. Each human cell contains 23 sets of chromosomes. We get one set of each of these chromosomes from each parent. Out of the 23 pairs, one pair is the sex chromosomes, which determine gender. For this testing, we focus on the remaining 22 pairs. These 22 pairs are called autosomes because they are found in all the cells. The DNA in these chromosomes is called autosomal DNA or atDNA.

Autosomal DNA (atDNA) is advantageous because it can be used to find out information about either lineage. This is because both males and females have autosomal DNA and we inherit autosomal DNA from both of our parents. So atDNA can be used to discover both our maternal and paternal lines. Fifty percent of our DNA is inherited from our mother and the other fifty percent from our father. Since our parents inherit 50% from each of their parents, we inherit half of that, which is 25% from our grandparents. As we go higher up the family tree, the DNA inherited is cut in half with each generation. Despite only having half of atDNA getting inherited at each step, there will be certain stretches or segments of atDNA that are preserved over numerous generations.

Autosomal DNA testing can be done either using SNPs or STRs. However, currently, SNPs are more commonly used than STRs. Both of them in their own right are useful for predicting ancestry. Similar to Y chromosome STRs, autosomal STRs are repeats of small DNA sequences. Because only 50% of DNA is inherited in each generation, the number of STR markers that are seen is reduced by half for each generation. Similarly, SNPs are single base substitutions in the genome. Autosomal DNA is mixed in every generation and hence the number of markers for SNPs is decreased by half. Hence, using the decreased number of SNPs to look for similar SNPs in previous generations companies figure out which family a person belongs to. The marker analysis can be matched in two ways. One is by using haploblock matching in which the number and size of similar DNA sequences is compared to existing samples. It helps in analyzing the closeness of a relationship. Another method is the biogeographical analysis. In this, the SNP markers are compared to reference values from populations of various ethnicity and geographical location. It can be used to pinpoint specific geographical locations and ethnicity ancestry for the patients.

This atDNA testing is done to compare your DNA on a broader level. The testers search for other DNA samples that have segments of atDNA similar to the patient's DNA. The smaller the common DNA sequences are, the longer back is the relationship between the two individuals. A statistical analysis is done to ascertain how similar the two atDNA samples are and if the similarity is strong, the two people are considered to be relatives. Depending on the percentage of similarity, the relationship can be determined. Higher percentages of similarity mean the closer the common ancestor is to the two patients. However, since the mixing of the atDNA is more than Y chromosome or mitochondrial DNA the predictability and accuracy reduces with an increasing number of generations. After five generations, the test is generally considered unreliable. Hence, it can be used to determine recent ancestry and not ancient ancestry. This testing can be used not only for determining birth parents or siblings or close relatives but also to determine ethnicity. Each ethnic group has their own specific mutations and DNA fragments that are unique to that group alone. Sometimes they can unique to an ethnic group living in a particular geographic location, which narrows down the search for relatives.

- ➢ Genealogy Software: - with the development in computer technology, multiple genealogy software has exploded in the market. These are used to collect, store, sort and display genealogical data.

- ➢ Study of records and documentation: - Genealogists also study records and documents like birth records, death records, marriage records, adoption records, census records, biographies, religious records and may more sources to find and gather information.

- ➢ Family names: - These are among one of the most important in studying a population. Family names usually directly indicate all the people who belong to the same family.

- ➢ Given names: - In many cultures people usually use names of their ancestors to name their children. This forms a repetitive pattern, hence names of ancestors can be found out with ease.

- Places name: - Often in many cultures people use the name of their place of origin in their name. This fact is exploited by genealogists to find out origin of a given family.

- Occupations: - Even today in many countries around the world people continue the same occupation as their ancestors like Potters, Masons etc. Hence, it is easy for genealogists to find ancestors.

There are various other sources that a genealogist may use to find ancestors and make a family tree.

Chapter 6: A Quick Look at Genealogy and Health Ailments

As discussed previously in this book, chromosomes are inherited by offspring from parents. As they inherit chromosomes they also inherit various health related problems like cancer, susceptibility to various diseases, allergies and many other health conditions that can be carried through the genes.

To avoid these unnecessary risks to the baby, parents usually consult a genetic counselor. These genetic counselors look at family history like cases of cancer, allergies, and all other inheritable genetic disorders.

The most often used method for this purpose is pedigree analysis. Pedigree analysis is a chart that is made to show the probability of inheritance of genetic conditions within a family. They are very important in determining whether an external characteristic is dominant, recessive or sex linked.

In case if a probability of a genetic disorder is expected in a fetus, either it is removed through surgery or proper medication can be used to maintain the health condition of the fetus. It totally depends upon the lethality of the disorder and the will of the parents.

Here are some diseases that are inherited and can be discovered if a pedigree analysis of the family tree is done.

Haemophilia

Hemophilia is a disease that slows down the blood clotting process. This disease becomes deadly when the infected person has a deep wound that is bleeding profusely. There are two types of hemophilia: hemophilia A and hemophilia B. The two types are similar with respect to signs and symptoms. However, the mutations, which cause each type, are different.

Hemophilia is more common in men than women because the disease follows a sex-linked inheritance. It is inherited through the X chromosome. It is an X-linked recessive trait. Since men have only one X chromosome, a single copy of the altered gene is enough to express the condition. Women, on the other hand, need to have two copies of the mutated gene for it to be expressed. A characteristic of this disease is that fathers cannot pass this disease onto their sons unless the mother is also a hemophiliac or a carrier. A carrier female is one who has a single copy of the mutated gene. Hence she will not express the disease but she will be able to pass it onto her children.

Hemophilia is caused by mutation in the genes F8 and F9. Mutation is F8 causes hemophilia A and mutation in F9 causes hemophilia B. There is another form of this disorder known as acquired hemophilia. This form is not inherited from parents. Instead it is characterized by recessive bleeding into the muscles, skin and other soft tissues. This form of the disease usually begins in adulthood. This disease results when the body produces proteins known as autoantibodies that disable the coagulation factor VIII, which further results in depletion of blood clotting proteins.

Let us talk about the inheritance of this recessive gene. As with any gene, there are two alleles. Since it is located on the X chromosome, let's consider two types of X chromosomes, one, which is mutated and labeled HX, and the normal one, which is X. Now since this is sex-linked, the inheritance varies depending on whether the progeny is male or female. If the mother is a carrier (^{H}XX) and the father is not affected (XY), then one daughter would be a carrier while one son would be infected while the other son and daughter would be normal. If the father is a hemophiliac (^{H}XY) and the mother (XX) doesn't carry the mutated gene, then none of the sons will have hemophilia while all the daughters will be carriers. If the father is a hemophiliac (^{H}XY) and the mother is a carrier (^{H}XX), 25% of their sons will be hemophiliac and the other 25% of their sons will be normal. 25% of their daughters will be hemophiliac while the remaining daughters will be carriers.

Sickle cell anemia

Sickle cell anemia is a disorder that affects the red blood cells (RBCs). It causes the body to produce a different type of hemoglobin called hemoglobin, which distorts red blood cells into a sickle cell shape instead of the usual round shape. This disease is inherited at birth. The symptoms of this disease manifest in childhood. Since the red blood cells are weirdly shaped, it leads to anemia, which further leads to frequent infections. When the RBCs distort, they break down easily and lead to anemia. This disease can cause severe pain when these sickle shaped RBCs get lodged in the blood vessels and obstruct the flow of blood. Hemoglobin has two parts: one alpha and one beta. Sickle cell anemia is caused by a mutation in one of the genes on chromosome 11 that is responsible for the development of the beta subunit of hemoglobin. As a result, the shape gets affected and these RBCs are not able to efficiently transport oxygen to various parts of the body.

Sickle cell anemia is a recessive autosomal disorder. Since, it isn't sex-linked, both males and females are prone to this disorder. Since it's a recessive disorder, a child will not inherit this disease unless both parents pass down a defective allele to the child. Children who inherit one defective and one normal allele are known to be carriers. While they don't have the disease they can transfer the disease to their offspring.

Sickle cell disease is caused by a mutation in the gene HBB. This gene helps in the making and development of the beta subunit of hemoglobin. A specific mutation of this gene leads to the production of an abnormal form of the beta-globin known as hemoglobin S. This mutation is the main cause of sickle cell anemia. There are other specific mutations that cause other diseases. With respect to sickle cell disease, at least one of the two beta subunits is replaced with the hemoglobin S form of the subunit. When this disease is inherited in the form of anemia, then both the subunits are mutated. In other variants, the beta subunits are replaced by both hemoglobin S and hemoglobin C, which is another mutant. Mutations in this gene can also lead to thalassemia.

The allele that codes for the mutated gene is represented as HbS while the normal allele is represented by HbA. HbS is a recessive trait and needs two allele copies for it to get expressed. Let's consider some scenarios of how the disease could be inherited. If one parent is homozygous dominant (HbAHbA) and the other is homozygous recessive (HbSHbS) then all the children would be carriers. However, if one parent is heterozygous (HbSHbA) and the other parent is homozygous dominant (HbAHbA) then none of the children would have the disease but half would be carriers. If both parents are heterozygous then 25% of their children would have the disease, 50% would be carriers and the remaining 25% would be normal.

Phenylketonuria (PKU)

Phenylketonuria is a disorder that leads to increased levels of phenylalanine in the blood. Phenylalanine is an amino acid that is found in our diet. It is found in all proteins and is used as an artificial sweetener. The body flushes out this phenylalanine because in concentrated amounts it is harmful to the body. PKU prevents the flushing out of this amino acid and hence leads to its accumulation in the blood. Accumulation of phenylalanine could lead to intellectual disabilities and other severe problems.

There are various forms of PKU depending upon the severity of the disorder. The most severe form of this disorder is known as classic PKU. Infants with this form appear to be normal for the first few months of their life. Soon they develop permanent intellectual disability, seizures, behavioral problems, psychiatric problems and delayed development. Children are also likely to have skin disorders and lighter color hair and skin as a result of excess phenylalanine in the body.

Variant PKU and non-PKU hyperphenylalaninemia are two other milder variants that have a lesser degree of brain damage. Children born to mothers with PKU have an increased risk of intellectual disability, heart defects and behavioral problems.

PKU is caused by mutations in the PAH gene. This gene is responsible for the production of an enzyme known as phenylalanine hydroxylase, which converts phenylalanine to other compounds required by the body. Mutation in this gene reduces the activity of this enzyme and hence phenylalanine gets accumulated in the body. This causes toxic effects in the tissue and blood. The nerve cells in the brain are extremely sensitive to levels of phenylalanine and because of this excessive amounts of this amino acid can lead to brain damage.

Classic PKU occurs when the enzyme activity is reduced or absent. Hence people with untreated classic PKU are prone to severe brain damage and behavioral problems. The other milder forms of PKU are caused by mutations that only slightly reduce the activity of the enzyme. This is why they are not as severe as classic PKU.

PKU is inherited as an autosomal recessive trait. This means that both alleles for the PAH gene need to be mutated for the disease to be expressed. Children who inherit only one mutated allele do not show any of the symptoms for this disease.

Let us consider that P denotes the dominant allele and p denotes the recessive allele. Let us now consider various situations of inheritance. If one parent is homozygous dominant (PP) and the other is homozygous recessive (pp), then all the children will have only one copy of the mutant gene which makes them carriers and hence they are not infected. If one parent is homozygous dominant (PP) and the other is heterozygous (Pp) then, 50% of their offspring will be normal and 50% will be carriers. However, if one parent is homozygous recessive (pp) and the other is heterozygous (Pp), 50% will be carriers and 50% will show symptoms of the disease. If both parents are heterozygous (Pp), then 25% will be normal, 50% will be carriers and the remaining 25% will have the disease. If both parents are homozygous recessive (pp) then all their children will inherit the disease from them.

Cystic fibrosis

Cystic fibrosis is a disease that causes thick, sticky mucus to clog and damage the organs in a body. It is an inherited disease whose common symptoms include extensive damage to the respiratory system.

Mucus is a slippery goo like substance that protects the linings of the stomach and other organs in the body. In people with this disease, the mucus becomes thick and sticky. This thick substance clogs airways, digestive tracts leading to respiratory and digestive problems. Over time, this leads to lung damage with scar tissue and cysts forming in the lungs.

Cystic fibrosis is a childhood disease that can now be managed with various treatments and therapies. Adults who develop this disease face digestive, respiratory and reproductive problems. Men who have cystic fibrosis have a defect in their vas deferens. Vas deferens are the tubes that carry the sperm. So when, this is blocked by mucus, sperm isn't carried for fertilization. Hence, men with cystic fibrosis will be infertile. Women with cystic fibrosis experience a lot of complications during pregnancy.

Cystic fibrosis is caused by a mutation in the CTFR gene on chromosome 7. This gene helps in the development of channels that transport chloride ions in and out of cells. The flow of chloride ions helps in the control of water movement in tissues, which is essential for the making of free flowing mucus. Mutations in this gene disrupt the functioning of these channels and hence prevent the regulation of chloride ions and water across membranes. This leads to the formation of thick mucus, which clogs the airways and ducts leading to organ damage.

Cystic fibrosis is an autosomal recessive disease. Hence, a person should have two copies of the mutated gene for the condition to get expressed. Let the normal allele be denoted by C and the mutant allele by c. Since this disease is a recessive disease, only if a person is homozygous recessive (cc) will they have the disease. Let's see how that can happen by considering various situations of inheritance. Consider two heterozygous parents (Cc) who are both carriers of the disease. Their children will have 25% homozygous dominant (CC), 25% homozygous recessive (cc) and 50% heterozygous (Cc). Hence only 1/4th of their children have a chance of inheriting the disease while ½ of their children have a chance of being carriers. If one parent is homozygous dominant (CC) and the other is homozygous recessive (cc), all their children will be carriers. If one parent is homozygous dominant (CC) and the other is heterozygous (Cc) then, their children have a 50% chance of being dominant and 50% chance of being carriers. If one parent is recessive (cc) and the other heterozygous (Cc), 50% of the children will be carriers and the remaining will inherit the disease.

Albinism

Albinism is a congenital disorder that is identified by the absence of pigments in the skin, eyes and hair due to defective tyrosinase. Tyrosinase is a copper-containing enzyme, which aids in the production of melanin. Albinism is a recessive disorder. A person without melanin is known as an albino while those with a reduced amount of the pigment are known as leucistic or albinoid. Albinism makes people more prone to sun burns and skin cancer. Melanin protects the body from the harmful UV rays of the sun. So, with the absence of melanin, albinos face a problem with increased risk of skin cancer and other diseases that are associated with overexposure to UV rays.

There are two types of this disorder: **Oculocutaneous** albinism (OCA) affects the eyes, hair and skin while **ocular** albinism (OA) affects only the eyes and not the hair and skin. Both these types cause eye defects.

There are two forms of albinism: the total absence of melanin is known as amelanism and a partial lack of the melanin is known as hypomelanism.

There are four types of oculocutaneous albinism and each of them is caused as a result of a single mutation in different genes. Type 1 is caused by the mutation in the gene TYR while type 2 is cause by the mutation of OCA2 gene. Type 3 is caused by a mutation in TYRP1 and a mutation in the gene SLC45A2 causes type 4 oculocutaneous albinism. All these four genes are used in the production of melanin. So, a mutation in these genes leads to absence of melanin or a reduction in the amount of melanin. Melanin also plays a role in vision in the retina. Type 2 oculocutaneous albinism is also characterized by a mutation in one other gene, the MC1R gene, which also helps in the regulation of melanin production. OA occurs due to a mutation in the X chromosome.

OCA is an autosomal recessive disorder. This means that only if a person inherits two recessive alleles will they be albino. So if a person has a heterozygous genotype then they will be carriers while those with homozygous dominant alleles will be normal. Hence, only if a person is homozygous recessive will they have the disease. Consider one parent is homozygous dominant and the other is homozygous recessive, all their children will be carriers. If one parent has the homozygous dominant alleles and the other is heterozygous then, their children have a 50% chance of being dominant and 50% chance of being carriers. If one parent is recessive and the other heterozygous, 50% of the children will be carriers and the remaining 50% will inherit the disease. If both the parents are heterozygous they will both be carriers and their children will 25% homozygous recessive, 25% homozygous dominant and 50% heterozygous.

OA is an X-linked recessive trait because of which it is more prevalent in men than women. Since it is transferred only through the X chromosome, women tend to be carriers unless the mother is also affected or if the mother is a carrier and the father is an albino. A carrier mother and an albino father will give to rise to the following possibilities: a carrier daughter or an OA daughter or an OA son or a normal son. If the mother has only the normal X chromosomes and the father has OA then 25% of the daughters have a chance of being a carrier while none of the sons will have the disorder.

Huntington's disease

Huntington's disease is a brain disorder that affects movement, emotions and cognition. The disease affects cells in the basal ganglia, which is the part of the brain that controls emotion, movement and cognitive ability. Adult-onset is the most common form of this disease which is surfaces in adults in their thirties or forties. Early symptoms of this disease include depression, poor coordination and slow learning skills. These people also develop twitchy or jerky movements. As this disease progresses, affected people have trouble speaking and walking. The life span for a person with adult-onset form of this disease is 15-20 years after the symptoms start.

Juvenile Huntington's disease is a less common form of this disease and it starts in childhood or adolescence. The symptoms for this form are very similar to adult-onset Huntington's disease. Additional symptoms of clumsiness, slurred speech and rigidity are observed in the juvenile form. Seizures occur in most of the children with this disease. This form of the disease progresses much faster than the adult-onset form and hence the life span is less than 15 years for children diagnosed with this disease.

Huntington disease is caused by a mutation in the HTT gene. This gene is involved in the production of the huntingtin protein. This protein is believed to play a major role in the neurons in the brain. The mutation that causes this disease includes a DNA fragment known as the CAG trinucleotide repeat. This fragment comprises of a series of cytosine, adenine and guanine, which appear numerous times in a row. Usually this CAG segment is repeated 10-35 times within the gene but for people with Huntington's disease, the segment is repeated up to more than 120 times. People with around 40 repeats may not develop the symptoms of this disease but those with more than 40 repeats always develop this disease. An increase in the size of this segment leads to a longer huntingtin protein, which is then cut, into smaller fragments that are toxic. These fragments accumulate in the neurons and disrupt the functioning of these cells in the brain. The eventual death of these neurons is the cause of all the symptoms of this disease.

Huntington's disease is an autosomal dominant trait. Being an autosomal dominant trait makes it easy to inherit this disease. Any person who has even a single copy of this gene is prone to this disease. Consider two alleles for the Huntingtin gene, one dominant (HTT) and one recessive (htt). The dominant allele is the one that could possibly code for the mutated gene. Since it is an autosomal dominant trait, both men and women are equally prone to this disease. When mutated copies of HTT exist in even one generation, there is a 50% chance that it will be transmitted to the next generation. Supposing one parent is homozygous dominant and the other is homozygous recessive, then all the children will have one mutated dominant allele, which makes them inherit the disease. If both parents are heterozygous, then 75% of their children will have a chance of inheriting the disease while they have a 25% chance of inheriting the recessive alleles.

The above diseases and disorders are just some of the many that can be inherited from the previous generations. Some of these diseases even skip a generation or two before they are expressed. Genetic counseling is a good way to realize whether you, as a parent, are a carrier for any of these diseases and taking the necessary precautions. While some of these diseases have a lesser chance of being inherited because they are recessive diseases, quite a few of them follow autosomal dominant inheritance which makes it very easy for the disease to be transmitted to your progeny.

Research in Genealogy

Today genealogy is an emerging field of research indulging many scientists, anthropologists and historians. Some of the major areas of research in the field of genealogy are as follows: -

- ➢ African American Research: - This area of research mainly focuses on the people who have African origin and are settled in America.

- ➢ Alien research: - This includes genetic analysis of humans and other primate species and trying to find out the possible genetic structure of the extra-terrestrials.

Software development: - As genealogical studies can also be software based, new software is being developed for better analysis and results.

Chapter 7 – Online Genealogy

As with most things in this day and age, there is a multitude of pay-for websites that are dedicated to helping you trace your family background. At the same time, which one is going to be the best one for your research and where do you begin?

Getting Started – Why Should You Go Online?

Online genealogy websites are incredibly popular due to one major aspect – simplicity. All you have to do is type in an ancestor's name into a search engine, click on the search button ad within seconds you will get hundreds of different websites presented to you. Many are free, a number are on a subscription basis, and some are pay on view, but when you see everything at once, it can be incredibly daunting, leaving you hanging your head down low wondering where on earth you start.

With so many subscription and pay per view websites out on the web, it can be a struggle to decide whether any of them are going to be worth it or not. Many of the websites where you have to pay for a service are most likely to be worthwhile but it is knowing whether it is going to be worthwhile to your own personal requirements. For those of you who are trying to figure out where to start regarding online genealogy, here are some helpful tips to help you get started.

When it comes to genealogy you are going to have to pay for the service. There is only so much you can do without having to punch in your credit card details. Offline, you would pay for private researchers, travelling to archive locations, libraries etc. This, and the cost of all of these other aspects, is why so many people are turning to genealogy websites to help them look for their ancestors.

The internet is inundated with material, more of which are being added to each day. Online genealogy is popular as people can access reliable and accurate information in a way that wasn't available in the past. Where a simple search could take several weeks or even months before, now it takes less than five minutes. When you take into consideration the cost of travelling to and from archives, memberships and time away from home and family, online research is far cheaper.

So which are the best free websites to start looking for your ancestors? The following is a short collection of free websites that are popular with genealogists.

www.freebmd.org.uk – features birth, marriage and death certificates for people in England and Wales.

www.familysearch.org – for international searches and run by the Church of Jesus Christ of Latter-Day Saints.

www.rootsweb.com – for genealogy information.

Do not expect to find everything that you need to know from

these websites because you won't. However, they will provide you with the building blocks to help you get started in building your personal family tree.

How to Choose the Right Site to Build Your Family Tree

There are certain principal details to be aware of before you start narrowing down your choice of websites.

Firstly, does it contain the fundamental sources of genealogy? At the very least, it should contain details of birth, marriage and death certificates, or provide the index to them, along with the census details. Without these details you are not going to get very far.

Secondly, does the website provide a full description as to what other details you can find on the website? Are you able to find the actual details of the records found on the website and how they can be utilized by researchers? If it doesn't, then it's going to be a struggle finding the details you will undoubtedly need.

Thirdly, are you able to view the original (or digitized) records or just the transcripts? The original documents, even in their digitized form, will always be better than a transcript, where someone has copied (and sometimes, miscopied) from. A number of websites will merely provide the indexes to these documents and you can simply order a copy of the original. In some cases, this is better because you will be able to see for yourself what is on the document when it arrives.

Fourthly, are you satisfied with the billing process? If you want a service where all the information and documents can be seen on the website, then a subscription package might be a better option for you. If you only need to see the information for a few documents, then it might be better to order on a pay per view basis.

The following is a selection of pay per view websites that are favored amongst genealogists.

www.genesreunited.co.uk – comprises birth, marriage and death indexes, along with census details covering England and Wales.

www.familyrelatives.com - comprises birth, marriage and death indexes, along with census details covering England and Wales.

www.ancestry.co.uk - comprises birth, marriage and death indexes, along with census details covering England and Wales.

www.findmypast.co.uk - comprises birth, marriage and death indexes, along with census details covering England and Wales.

www.scotlandspeople.gov.uk - comprises birth, marriage and death indexes, along with census details covering Scotland.

Dig Down Deeper

Once you have the basic details of your family and have created a minimal family tree, it is time to get out your virtual shovels and start digging down deeper. This is where more specialized genealogy websites start coming in. These include church records, military records, wills etc. However, you will need the essential information to make the most out of these types of websites. For example, if you are looking to discover more information on your great-grandfather's naval career then you're not going to get far if you don't even know his name and when he was born, are you? This background information is of great importance – without it you won't be able to distinguish your great-grandfather's information from the thousands of others out there. Clearly, it is essential that you are utilizing the genealogy websites in the right way to get what you need to get from them.

With so many websites out there, many will share certain characteristics and information. You may want to ask the following when viewing them:

Does the website feature the information which is essential to your ancestor? For example, if your great-grandmother was part of a foreign diplomat team, does the website feature the documents related to her during the years that she was employed in such a role?

Does the website describe the records and documents featuring on the website? It is especially annoying to pay to see if you can access any relevant details on a website, so it is a good idea to find out whether the website offers a description of what types of documents and records the website holds. This way, you can see if you are likely to find any information regarding your ancestors' identities.

Does the website feature any examples of the various kinds of documents found on it? From these examples, you can get an idea as to whether they will be helpful in finding the type of information needed for your personal search.

Does the website feature the contact details for a behind the scenes person to liaise with in case you have any questions or queries regarding your search?

The following is a small selection of pay for websites that are favored amongst genealogists:

www.nationalarchives.gov.uk – the website features many types of specialized documents including World War One Campaign Medal index, naval records, wills and many others.

www.originsnetwork.com – the website features numerous specialized records and documents for British ancestry including military records, marriage indexes, wills and apprenticeship details.

Hittp://archive.timesonline.co.uk – this website features documents surrounding famous, infamous or wealthy people between 1798 and 1985.

Although many specialized websites do charge for some records, there are numerous websites on the internet which cost nothing. The Commonwealth War Graves Commission website (www.cwgc.org) is great for finding out the details of the men and women in the military who died during World War One and World War Two.

However, if you cannot find the information you need online then it is most likely time to head off to the archives. Not every type of records and documents can be found on the internet, so keep in mind that no matter how long you search online, you may find yourself in the archive halls anyway. However, online genealogy websites are a great starting point.

The Other Types of Websites You Can Use

Tracing your family line doesn't mean just simply searching for names and dates on a simple search engine database – there are numerous other types of websites that you can use to bring your ancestry to life! These include databases, support websites, forums, display tools and so many others. However, unless you desperately need particular details from a past record, then it's not necessary to pay out for these websites. Try looking at the following selection of websites that could offer you different information whilst you are searching for your past:

www.cyndislist.com – this website features numerous information and links to other websites regarding genealogy.

www.genuki.org.uk – this website features numerous articles, advice and tips on genealogy.

What Types of Records Can You Expect to Find?

Depending on where your ancestors come from, or where living, will determine what type of records you are most likely to come across. Certain websites, such as www.findmypast.co.uk, are great when it comes to English, Welsh and Irish records in particular. They boast on having the biggest collection of military records on the internet, as well as holding a comprehensive collection of Irish and Church parish records. It is the only website which features the 1939 Register, which fills in the census hole which occurred between 1921 and 1951.

Many websites will update their record archives on a regular basis, sometimes weekly, and this does not impact on the cost that current subscribers pay already.

You may also come across old newspapers online, many dating from the early 18th century right into the 20th century. These are a great addition to your online search as they really add a distinctive and unique insight into individuals' lives.

What Kind of Specialized Websites Can You Expect to Find?

Many genealogy websites have started to offer specialized records to their subscribers, which is particularly useful if an ancestor worked in a particular profession. The following is a list of the types of specialized documents you may need to access at some point:

Merchant Navy Seaman Records

British in India Records

British Army Service Records (18th – 20th centuries)

Bank of England Wills Extracts (18th – 20th centuries)

British Royal Air Force Service Records

What Else Will You Find?

Many websites feature an easy to use family tree builder so that you can visualize your ancestors in a simple yet effective way. Each individual is typically given their own page where you can upload photos, document scans and even audio clips if you have any. Some family tree builders even feature a kind of calculator where it calculates what the relationship is between you and another individual.

Numerous websites will offer you suggestions to who might be related to you, based on certain criteria you have already input in your tree and profile.

Now Where to Begin?

Each website will differ as to how many documents they will hold but most feature around two to three billion records and documents, with more being added to on a regular basis. As such, it should be easy enough to start building your family tree, leaf by leaf.

What Do You Know Already?

The best way to get started is by jotting down everything that you are aware of already. At this point, just use the facts and not what gossip is going around in the family. This should include names, dates of births, marriage dates, divorce dates, dates of deaths etc. It doesn't matter if you don't know a lot of information, but if you know something then you can simply start your tree with just your own name and date of birth.

Once you have your basic details, start talking with the other members of your family in order to see what you can find out from them. Some of the best research you can do is simply by talking to other family members. In addition to the bare facts, the stories they can tell can really brighten up your search and make it more inspirational than before.

However, it is a good idea to make sure you have detailed notes to fall back on at times. Keep a record of the key dates and facts someone has told you about and note down who it was who told you the information.

What Kind of Questions Should You Ask?

- What is their full name? Did they like to use a middle name instead of their given name? Or did they use a nickname?
- What was their date of birth?
- Where were they born?
- Who were their parents? Were they married? Did they divorce later on?
- Did the individual ever get married? Where did they live? Where did they get married?
- What was the name of their spouse?
- Did they have children, either in or out of wedlock?
- Did they lose any of their children?
- What were their names and dates of birth?
- What were their occupations?
- What religious denomination did they belong to?
- What schools did they go to? What degrees, if any, did they hold?
- What original documents/records are available, such as marriage, birth or death certificates?
- Are there any photographs or other depictions of them? Are there any newspaper clippings available?

Have a Look in the House

You will be surprised as to what information is laying in your house waiting for it to be uncovered. Start your online genealogy search by looking for original documents and records in your house itself. This can include birth certificates, marriage and/or divorce certificates or anything relating to a past occupation.

Old photographs, letters, newspaper clippings, scrapbooks, heirlooms – all of these are great ways to help you get started. Perhaps one of your ancestors wrote dates, names or any other details on the back of items. Bibles are a great way of tracing a family tree as it was popular with both British and American families in the past to write down the names of family members in the family Bible. As such, these family Bibles are a great reference when tracing a family tree.

Widening the Search

Sometimes it can be hard to find any information on your ancestors and as a result, you may need to widen your search. Numerous genealogy websites offer various new paths for which you can use to see if you can find any new information. Try looking on military records – they usually hold the records for all personnel who served both in their home countries and abroad, particularly since the mid-18th century.

Consular records are a great source of information. Perhaps one of your ancestors was posted overseas and this is why your search has hit a dead-end? The National Archives holds the Passenger Lists for British citizens who made long-haul journeys to distant lands between the late 19th century and the middle of the 20th century.

Chapter 8 – Where to Look for Your Ancestors

Birth, Marriage & Death, including Parish

In the United Kingdom, civil registration began in 1837. For births, marriages and deaths (along with various other information), it could be found in the parish records. Even today, these parish records are highly vital when it comes to tracing back your family tree. Parish records can stretch back as far as 1538.

The civil registration can be looked at online, dating from 1837 to 2005 and are typically known as the BMD index collection. All you do is simply type in the name or any other data you may have and click. Many genealogy websites relating to the United Kingdom will have online access to the Parish Registers where you can discover all the details regarding to baptisms, marriages and deaths.

The reason why these three key information points are so important is that our birth, our weddings and our deaths are the main occasions which happen in our lives. The civil registration maintains that information and are usually held by a civic authority; they give you more insight into your ancestors, allow you to separate your ancestor from others who bore the same name and give you new leads into searching for new family members, both deceased and living.

Search Tips

When you register a new birth, marriage or a death, a certificate is completed and then the information is added to a file and then transferred onto the summary register, also known as the Index, of the occasion. You may not be able to find out all the information from these Indexes, but the main information – such as names, date of birth, other dates, locations etc. – will be there for you to read. In addition to this, you will probably find references of how to order a copy of the certificate.

It is imperative that once you have found the record of your ancestor that you order a Birth, Marriage or Death certificate (a BMD certificate). You can order these online at any of the ancestry websites. If you are looking for an ancestor in the United Kingdom before 1837 then you need to look under the UK Parish Baptism, Marriage and Burial Records. Again, this will be accessible online. Once you have ordered a certificate, it will be sent to you in the post.

Census Records

When searching for an ancestor from the United Kingdom, the best starting point is the 1911 Census which then backdates ever 10 years until 1841. These census records will be able to tell you where they lived, where they were born, name, gender, how old they were when the census took place, their occupation and even who they were living or staying with when it took place!

After 1851, the Census records also recorded who the individual was in relation to the head of the household, whether they were married and if they suffered from any disabilities.

When it comes to the 1911 census records, it is particularly thrilling to read because the individual could write their personal information down in their own hand. Sometimes, they even added personal comments.

Census records are a goldmine of information as for more than a century all those who were living in the country could be traced. You are able to weave a family tree that stretches back centuries and find out who they were, what they did and where they came from.

Search Tips

The census was designed to keep track of who was staying in the house when the census was being recorded that day, which did include strangers, travelers and family members. When it comes to tracing someone who may not have lived permanently in that house, once you have discovered their location on a map from the information on the census, then you can look for churches, graveyards and other locations where they may have left information.

Also, trace the individual's siblings in the census records as many extended family members would live together in one residence. This way you could find grandparents, aunts, uncles, cousins, step-siblings and many others either living in the same house or close-by.

If you are having difficulty in trying to trace your ancestor, then just use a first name and date of birth or the place of birth instead.

Sometimes, the census records will only write in the initials of the person instead of their full name. In addition to this, some of the census takers did not always have the best handwriting so if you are having trouble trying to locate someone, try using just the initial or an initial that looks similar to their real one.

Ships in either British waters or in port were counted separately from 1851. Census records for crew members in 1841 and 1851 were not filled out so information retaining to crew members only began in 1861 and recorded on special shipping schedules.

Immigration and Travel Information

Immigration and naturalization records are a great source of information and map out the gigantic decision to move to a different country and start a new life there. Unfortunately, there is not much of the way of information when it comes to these types of records but they are vital in the way of being able to trace a big step in their journey. They are another piece of the puzzle and you may learn more about the travelling conditions of that time.

The immigration and travel records from the 20th century onwards contain much more detail compared to the earlier records, usually containing the details of other family members in both the original country and the new one. In addition to this, you should also find the individual's occupations, last address, and place of birth and sometimes even a photograph.

Many online genealogy websites will have access to the immigration and travel records. Items in these collections usually include naturalization records, passports, passenger arrival records, medical records, convict records and emigration information. You may learn where your ancestors originally came from, whom they travelled with and where they travelled onto.

Search Tips

When searching for your ancestor through immigration and travel records it is best if you have their name, date of birth or age, when they arrived, the departure point, port of arrival and the country of origin.

Depending on where your ancestor may have come from, it is possible that they may have spelled their name wrong or have used an English version and that the surname may have an ethnic variant. You may want to try and learn some of the various ethnic spellings of the surname so you can try searching for your ancestor in their native language.

When it comes to immigration and travel records you should always look at the first copy of it as it is possible it contains more information than other later copies. This may include their intended address once in the new country, any relatives in the country or even the details of those they were travelling with. Should you find any notes such as an Index collection or another reference detail that isn't connected with the first copy, then the collection online should have the link where you can find the details on how to access the original certificate.

One important tip to remember is to jot down any names who were witness or another passenger from the same destination on these records. Many times these people were relatives, friends or occupational acquaintances from their original homelands. It is possible that you could find out more information pertaining to your ancestor's life before they embarked on their journey and afterwards through the information you find in either census or immigration/travel records.

UK Incoming Passenger Lists, 1878-1960

The UK Incoming Passenger Lists is an index to the passenger lists compiled by the Board of Trade. Here, all foreign ships from ports outside of Europe and the Mediterranean were expected to provide the details of those sailing on-board. Ships which were exempt from this rule were those from outside these areas but then arrived in Mediterranean or European ports to collect passengers; some of the ships' final port of call was not even the United Kingdom.

Whilst the UK Incoming Passenger Lists originate in 1878, many of the earlier records were actually destroyed by the Board of Trade so some of the information may have been lost. However, the rest of the records continue up to 1960.

There were two distinctive lists – one for British and Commonwealth subjects and another list for all other foreigners (also referred to as Aliens). The forms changed frequently over the decades so a search in this database may turn up a range of different information for individual passengers.

Australian Convict Transportation Registers – 1791-1868

The Australian Convict Transportation Registers is the index compiled regarding to convicts who were sent to Australia. From the 17th century onwards, convicted criminals were transported to various points in the British Empire. At first it was to America but when the American Revolutionary War broke out in 1776 a new penal colony was established in Australia. The first ship of convicts sent to Australia was launched in 1787, the second in 1789 and the third in 1791. Although the convict ships were officially stopped in 1868, none had actually been sent out for around ten years beforehand. It is estimated that around 160,000 people were transported to Australia in that time.

The Australian Convict Transportation Registers is accessible online and the information will typically contain: the convict's name, date and place of conviction, sentence details, the ship's name, when it departed and the colony destination.

You should be aware that not all the convict ships departing from England were recorded and whilst an ancestor may have been on board one of these convict lists, the degree of record keeping was not great.

U.S. and Canada, Passenger and Immigration Lists Index, 1500s-1900s

For American searchers looking for ancestors who arrived

from another country, the Passenger and Immigration Lists Index is the best source of information, particularly for those whose ancestors arrived before the 19th century. The index can be accessed online and has records of nearly five million people who landed on American and Canadian soil from the 16th to the 20th century, making it the best place to start your search.

Trying to decipher passenger lists can be quite boring and dull but the Passenger and Immigration Lists Index is quite simple and fast to navigate through. All the entries can be searched by a keyword and are indexed by name. Before 1820, those who ventured the dangerous trip to America would sail on ships in small numbers (between five and 30 typically) and the majority of the ships didn't actually keep good records of whom was on board. As a result, documentation of your ancestor's voyage to America before the early 19th century is extremely difficult for most searchers.

Because of this, the Passenger and Immigration Lists Index is vital for searching for ancestors arriving to America before 1820 because it is compiled over thousands of different records. It is updated every year as more information is found and added to.

The New York, Passenger and Immigration Lists, 1820-1850

The New York Passenger and Immigration Lists is compiled of the records of around 1.6 million people who departed foreign ports and landed at New York from 1820 to 1850. For many reasons, including to help reduce overcrowding on passenger ships, Congress brought about a rule in 1819 to police these ships. As a result, all passenger ships were obliged to produce a list of all on board and handed to the collector of customs when the ship docked in port.

This new rule also included that the collector of customs was to hand over passenger lists four times a year to the Secretary of State, which was then given to Congress. After this, the information from these lists was then published as Congressional documents.

The UK Royal Navy Medical Journals, 1817-1857

The UK Royal Navy Medical Journals are an index of images from medical journals which were recorded aboard British ships from the 19th century. These journals were penned by the medical officers on board who were obliged to keep a record of all patients' details, including their treatments and the results whilst on board. There are 61 volumes within this index and are from a range of ships although high proportions are from convict ships heading to Australia.

The UK Royal Navy Medical Journals hold a wealth of information that you may overlook initially. Most records will give you their name, their 'quality' (the rank of the patient), any diseases, notes on symptoms, treatments and how long their treatment lasted for. In addition to this, they also record all those who were sick – not just patients but passengers and crew; details on those who died en route; and they provide valuable information on how people were medically treated.

The Slave Registers of former British Colonial Dependencies, 1813-1834

The Abolition of Slave Trade Act began in 1807, making the slave trade from Africa to all British colonies illegal. In order to fight against the illegal transportation after the Act was enforced, the majority of British colonies started to produce a list of all black slaves who had been "lawfully enslaved". The Office for the Registry of Colonial Slaves was set up in London 1819 and all the slave lists were forwarded here, usually updated every three years or so. The registers were kept right up to when slavery was abolished in 1834.

This collection consists of the slave registers for many colonies, mainly in the Caribbean, Mauritius and Sri Lanka and gives the following information: the name of the slave (if they had been baptized then this usually included both a Christian name and their given name), their age, gender, name of owner, name of residence and their nationality.

The St. Croix, U.S. Virgin Islands, Slave and Free People Records, 1733-1930

The St. Croix Slave and Free People Records consist of a range of documents and other records which chronicle the key events of slaves and free people in St. Croix. This island was home to a variety of settlers (British, French, Spanish, Dutch and Carib to name but a few) prior to being bought by the Danish in 1733. Sugar was the main production right up to the 19th century and slaves were brought to the island in order to provide the manpower at the sugar plantations. In 1848, slavery was abolished and the island was bought by the United States in 1916 and became one of the US Virgin Islands. The documents contained in the Slave and Free People Records are quite diverse and includes slave lists, medical journals, census records, tax lists, immigration lists, free men of color militia lists, marriages, deaths and burials, plantation records, school registers and many others. The information provided by these records will vary greatly.

The U.S. Virgin Islands Census, 1835-1911 (Danish Period)

During the Danish period, the island of St. Croix produced several census records which can be accessed through this collection. Again, the information produced will vary greatly but may contain their name, age, household number, status (whether freed or slave), gender, marital status, children, religion, birthplace, how they are related to the head of the household, and whether they owned slaves or not.

Military Records

Military records are a goldmine of information but it is important that you know when and where a soldier had once served and if they were an officer or in the enlisted ranks. You may be able to find out this kind of information by talking with family members, going through old photos, journals, diaries or even through any medals locked in a box in the attic. Military records were produced both in times of peace and in war, subject to the type of document, and it is possible that you may find documents relating to an ancestor who were drafted but never actually served. This includes the US World War I Draft Registrations were 24 million men were recorded but were never sent to war.

The documents found in these collections, accessible from certain genealogy websites, consist of a variety of information including service records, draft records, enlistment dates and pension information. It can also help you start to learn more about the heroes in your family and those who surrounded, loved and supported them.

WWI Records

World War I has had a huge impact on the majority of families in the United Kingdom and many of European countries. There is a wealth of records and collections to aid you in your search for ancestors who lived and died during this period.

Service records

Service records are probably the best starting point when it comes to searching for information during WWI. These service records are a collection of documents which are created during the lifetime of a person's career in the military and will generally include their registration details, personal details (such as eye color, hair color, height etc.), regiment details, ranks, main event dates and any injuries.

Many genealogy websites will have at least one collection pertaining to service records during WWI. One collection will consist of the records of those who died during the war and those who served until the war was finished in 1918. It should be stressed though that some of these documents were destroyed during WWII but even still, the collection has more than two million individuals.

A second collection is usually made up of the records pertaining to the soldiers who were discharged during the war, the majority of which suffered injuries. After they were discharged, the Pension Office would calculate what the soldier was allowed to receive.

Service records are a great starting point since they are quite easy to navigate and will include a good amount of information, including names, age, birthplace, regimental number etc.

Medal records

Everyone who participated in World War One would be presented with at least one medal; the majority of soldiers were likely to receive around four medals. Each meal was earned due to particular circumstances, at certain locations or for outstanding bravery.

The WWI Medal Rolls Index Cards is a great way of learning whether your ancestor earned any medals during this dark, bloody time in history. In this index you will discover the records of what medals each of the five million men who served in the war earned during his career. You will most likely need your ancestor's regimental number since many soldiers bore the same name. In addition to this, the index is also separated into sections devoted to specific medals, such as the Silver War Badge Collection, the Citations of the Distinguished Conduct Medal and the Naval Medal and Award.

Other records

There is a great deal of other record collections that can help you trace the history of your ancestor during the Great War, particularly for those who sacrificed their lives. The De

Ruvigny's Roll of Honour Index is a list of all those who died and contains biographies (including photographs most of the time) of nearly 30,000 men from the Armed Forces. The British Commonwealth War Graves Registers can help you located where your ancestor may have been laid to rest, containing the information of about 250 cemeteries.

World War II records

When comparing a search between WWI documents and WWII documents, it is quite easy to say that you may find the availability of service records severely limited for the latter. This is because many of the service records are still in the hands of the Ministry of Defense and, as such, are still classified. However, don't despair because there are many collections and indexes which can help you find out information on your ancestors who served during WWII.

If one of your ancestors serviced in the British military and died during the conflict, then they should be named into the UK Army Roll of Honour 1939 – 1945. If you search their name and find the right individual (remember, many soldiers bore the same name) then you should be able to discover certain information including when they died, how they died, the regiment they served in, where they died in and their branch. Unfortunately, since the information is contained within transcripts by the National Archives there is no original document but the details are still there for you.

Another free collection of WWII documents to search is the UK Army Pensioners of War Index. During the war, many soldiers were captured by the enemy and held in camps of war. If your ancestor was in one of these camps, this collection can tell you when they were captured, their rank, regiment details, prisoner numbers, the location of the camp and the type of camp.

For Jewish ancestors who were fortunate to survive the Holocaust then you can start searching for them in the Sharit Ha-Platah 1946, which contains the names and details of more than 60,000 survivors.

Even if much of the military service records are still held by the Military of Defense then you are able to request a copy of them by sending a letter to them. If the person is still alive then you will need to gain their permission, or the permission of their nearest living family member.

Chapter 9 – Useful Advice in Searching for Your Ancestors

Ten common research mistakes

There will be times when you will make mistakes when searching for your ancestors. Just think of any mistakes as learning curves. Let's take a look at the top ten common mistakes you may make when researching for your family tree.

1 – Disorganization

When you are tracing your family tree it is important that you stay as organized as possible. When you forget to keep your information up-to-date then it is incredibly easy to lose important information. You can download software online to keep all the details in one place and there are forms that you can use as well. By keeping the information and documents you find organized, not only do you help yourself, but anyone else who wants to join in the search in the future.

2 – Ignoring any siblings

It is very easy to focus on one name but if you limit your search too much then you may lose out on discovering a great deal of information. When you look at records such as census records, you may discover not only your ancestor's name, but the names of their siblings, parents, grandparents, aunts, uncles, cousins etc. Tracing the name of a sibling could lead to you a living relative of their descendants who are tracing their family tree too. In addition to this, it is confirmation that you are on the right track.

3 – Not noting down your female ancestor's maiden names

It is quite easy to overlook one particular detail when researching female ancestors – their maiden names. All too often, you will focus on their married names and miss out on all the information their maiden names can tell you. This includes the maiden names as part of a name for their children and can also help you locate the correct male ancestor when there is more than one person with the same name at the same location and date.

4 – Believing you are related to someone famous

Even if you have the same surname of someone famous, either present or in the past – it doesn't necessarily mean that you are a relation and start waiting for a dinner invitation. This is certainly a mistake that some researchers will make, trying to connect a famous person to themselves through a family tree. This is only going to lead to you trouble. The best way to trace your family tree is by starting with yourself and slowly making your way back through the past with each generation. If you do find someone famous in your tree, then you can start shouting about it!

5 – Jumping too far back

Many families will have several members who bear the same name, usually a boy given the same name as a respected father or grandfather. This can be quite confusing for some but for others it's not seen as important and so an individual is often overlooked for an older generation. Try not to do this as you lose out on knowing about their individual personality and place in the family. Do concentrate on their key dates and events and record them carefully in order to avoid confusion.

6 – Assumptions on surnames

Your surname offers a wealth of information regarding your family history but do not make the assumption that your surname was always spelt that way. In the past, surnames were often misspelt and altered depending on the circumstances of that time. For instance, Smith could be changed to Smyth, Peyton to Payton, and Lee to Leigh. When searching, try varying the way your surname is spelt as sometimes this will result in more information.

7 - Jumping to conclusions and not landing on the right information

Like archaeology, you need to have proof when it comes to genealogy. When you link one generation with the next you must have a link that is backed up with evidence (this can include birth certificates, marriage documents etc.); many times mistakes are made when someone jumps to a conclusion based on feelings or a hunch and does not land on the right information. If you are not 100% certain on a connection, instead of saying that this is fact just make a note of what you think and then try to prove it. Do not assume anything.

8 – Searching for the wrong people

This particular mistake happens quite regularly; especially if you are making mistake number seven (see above). If you do not have the right connection, then it's quite possible that you will jump family trees and start researching the wrong family. This is why it is vital that you have a secure connection from one generation to the next.

9 – Basing all information from the internet

There is no doubt that the internet is a great place to begin searching for all your lost ancestors; however, many genealogy websites are massive and hold links to vast collections and indexes from all over the world. Some websites are not as reliable as others and even the smallest inaccuracy relating to an individual can have a big impact on someone else researching their family tree. When you have found a source that gives you information and you are unsure of it, be cautious and try to prove that it's reliable.

10 – Not documenting all documents

Organization is key when it comes to researching your family but even more so is by recording where you found your information from. Remember, you may be researching your family now but if another member of your family decides to join in the quest then it is important that they don't make any of the previously mentioned mistakes. So that they don't make mistake number seven, record where your records were found. This is part of your legacy, remember.

A Guide to Old Photos

Old photographs discovered in a dusty trunk in the attic or hidden away in a century old diary or even tucked away in a military file – old photographs really bring history to life and when it is a part of your family, there are no words to describe the excitement of seeing an ancestor with your own two eyes (even if it is just a snapshot in time). However, a photograph can tell you so much more than simply what a person looked like. Knowing what type of photograph, you have to hand can help confirm whether the individual in it is actually your ancestor or not as different types of photographs can tell you when it was taken.

Daguerrotypes

Daguerreotypes were produced between 1839 and 1860 and were made from silver plated copper with a surface which was polished that it shone brilliantly. These types of old photographs were extremely delicate and were typically placed in small velvet padded cases.

Tintypes or Ferrotypes

Tintypes, also known as Ferrotypes, were frequently produced between 1856 and the early 20th century, but were extremely popular during the U.S. Civil War. These types of old photographs consist of an image imprinted into a thin iron sheet which was then painted with black varnish. They were popular because they were much more flexible and wouldn't break when soldiers posted them home to loved ones.

Cabinet Cards

If you find an old photograph dating from the late 19th century and early 21st century, then it is likely to be known as a cabinet card. A cabinet card was a photo printed onto paper and then fixed to a piece of thicker card. The studio or photographer's name was usually printed on the back.

After the beginning of the 21st century, the majority of portraits were printed onto paper fixed to a postcard back, quite similar to how most postcards are designed today. They were popular until around the 1920s.

Questioning Your Relatives

Once you have documented your basic details, it can be hard to know where to start tracing the lives of your family. Your best bet is to start questioning your living family. In just half an hour you may be able to discover little known facts, vibrant characters you've never heard of and be enthralled with stories you weren't aware of. Read on for the best ways to question your family.

Talking to the older generation

It is important that you start talking to the older generation as soon as possible. A high number of us will start becoming interested in our family history when we are older and by this time the older generation has either passed on or may be struggling with disorders like dementia or Alzheimer's. As a result, the information they can provide is sadly lost. Start asking questions whilst you can; the older generation can usually give you information on two or three generations back. Also, talk to other members of your family as some are given more information than others over the years.

Overcoming hesitancy to offer information

The majority of the time you should be able to find out parts of your family that you didn't know before but there may be times when some members may be hesitant in sharing what they know. This could be regarding the birth of a baby before the parents were married, a cross-cultural relationship, a runaway teen, someone with a criminal past etc. If you should come across family members who are reluctant in sharing information, sit them down and explain why you are looking into the family tree and how their information could greatly help. Offer to share anything you discover as talking about a long-lost relative can make them curious about what happened afterwards.

Research your questions

Whilst it is important to prepare the questions that you want to ask, it doesn't mean that you have to read them out like a military questionnaire. Try to relax as you ask your relatives about what information they have, or if it is someone you don't know well (or at all), ask them in a casual manner. Ask whether you can call them back another time if you need to.

Types of questions to put forth

It's all very well going up to a relative and saying point blank, "what was your grandmother's name and when was she born?" Whilst they are good questions you are likely to get a short, sharp response and that is that. However, if you say, "I'm really getting into tracing the family tree. Can you tell me about your grandmother and anything you remember about her?" then you are more likely to get more details and make your relative feel useful and reflect on their relationship. If you have any old photographs, show them to your relatives as this can help job old memories that may have been put aside mentally. Ask them questions in a friendly manner to explain their connections with each other and this will certainly bring new color and vibrancy to your search.

Discovering family records

Whilst you are talking with your relatives, ask them if they have any old records or documents that you could take a look at. If they don't possess them see if you can find out who does; this goes for old photographs too, which could have been given to a different family member.

True or false?

Whether it is deliberate or not, there may be times when the information you gain may not be 100% accurate. However, don't despair because you can use this as a base from which you search. Always fact check all the details you find, especially on the internet; family stories are often adapted, changed, modified and altered for several reasons and not everyone's memories will stay sharp over long periods of time, so it is vital that your information is as accurate as you can determine.

Top Tips for What to do When You Hit a Brick Wall

There will be times when you're searching for an ancestor and suddenly find yourself stuck. Where do you go? What do you do? Read on for the top tips for what you should do when you hit a brick wall.

Reassess Your Information

Your very first step is to stop and take a look on how you have reached this point in your research. Reassessing all your information is a highly practical thing to do for several reasons. Firstly, you will find it refreshing to see exactly how much information you have gained over the period of time you've been searching and help you gain perspective for searching for that obscure ancestor you are having difficulty with. For example, many times researchers will unknowingly overlook a piece of information – it could be a vague reference to another family member on a census record or two people with names which sound or look alike on a birth, marriage or death certificate – but going back and retracing your work could suddenly thrust these names into the light. Reassessing your work allows you to see if you have overlooked any information the first time around or if you have made a mistake somewhere.

Many times researchers have hit a dead end because they did not verify information from an earlier generation. Question everything that you believe about the ancestor, especially if you haven't found concrete evidence and are basing your knowledge on hearsay, as many times the information you've found is incorrect. Check and then double check everything – dates of birth, place of birth, residence, marriage dates, sibling names, parent names and, importantly, spellings. If you have been simply going by on information given to you by family, now is the time to find definite proof.

Utilize All Sources Available

Many times you can get pass this brick wall simply by extending your search perimeters. You start by looking through every type of record, document and other information for that individual – census records, birth, marriage and death certificates, military records etc., and ensure that you are able to get copies of every single one as well. Look at each one and see if you can find any notes, names, dates, references etc. If you have everything but still can't find anything, then your next step is to extend your search.

Start by seeing if your ancestor was a passenger on a foreign ship – Passenger List collections are a great source of information and may explain why you can't find them. Search through different trade indexes, parish records, military service rolls etc.

Different Spellings

The more you travel back in time, the more likely you will run into different spellings of both given name and surnames. It wasn't so long ago that literacy levels were not that high and sometimes names were spelt how they were heard, especially if it was an unusual name. Those people who could not spell their names to the recorders would not be able to read their names to see if it was spelled correctly. Names were often spelt different and up until the Victorian era, were spelled how they sounded. If you are looking for an ancestor before the mid-19th century, then remember to take this into account.

Sometimes the change in names is deliberate. Some people, especially those coming from foreign locations, would change it to blend in better with those in the new country. Others may deliberately change their names in order to break contact with a past life.

Age Discrepancies

Many times it will be a name that makes you hit a dead end but sometimes it is the age which is the contributing factor. There were many reasons why an incorrect age will be noted on a document – sometimes the recorder has inadvertently written the wrong age or date of birth but sometimes the individual will give a false age. Maybe they wanted to join the army but were too young (or too old); perhaps they wanted to marry someone much older or younger than themselves and believed that by changing their age this helped reduce the gossip, or sometimes they were escaping from a dangerous and/or abusive individual and by altering certain key information they could hide. In addition to this, sometimes people did not know their exact date of birth and one was given to them based on how old they looked or acted.

The downside to this is that one piece of inaccurate information can lead to other details being wrong or harder to discover. Try to double check all dates of birth and ages and compare each document to others.

Look at Other Individuals

Even if you've tried everything suggested above and still hit a brick wall please don't throw in the towel. The following step may help you in finding the path to that ancestor.

Instead of focusing on that one individual, try looking at the different branches of your family tree. Look at siblings of the previous generation, aunts, uncles, cousins. You don't always have to have to focus on your direct ancestor to trace your ancestry; your wider family ancestors are all as equally important. Not only that, but sometimes it takes taking a step back and looking at another line to help you discover that direct ancestor. These types of family members are what is known as collateral kin.

It may appear that collateral kin may not be as important as a direct ancestor but at certain points in history a kinship was extremely important. Although your grandmother's siblings or cousins may not be close family members to you today, a few centuries ago this would have been very different.

When you start researching the collateral kin, you may find they bring you back to your original search. Census records, as we previously discussed, would record all those who stayed in the house the night before so it could be that your direct ancestor was staying at another relative's house the night before the census was taken. It could be that another family member left them something in their will or be a witness on a marriage certificate or other official record. In addition to this, it was quite common for cousins to marry.

Know Your History

Another point to be aware of is to remember that your family history is connected with what was going on during their time. Major events during their lifetime would have had an impact on your ancestor's personal life and genealogy has a way of bringing that past back to life.

If you knew that your ancestor was a young man during the 1910s then it is quite likely that they may have fought during the Great War. Military service records and other record collections are a good place to start. It is believed that around 250,000 teenage boys joined up for the army when they were underage and around 120,000 of them died during the war. Their military and death certificates are most likely to say the ages they claimed they were instead of their actual ages since they lied when registering.

Say you have your ancestor's name, age, location and death certificate. That's great, but what does it tell you about their lives between birth and death? What did they do? Where did they relocate to and why? What was going on at the time? Was there a revolution and they fled to escape the carnage?

Knowing the historical events of the day can help you ask questions to help you search for your ancestors, particularly the ones finding hard to trace. You may discover your ancestor in an old newspaper article, or find them in minor politics. It will also help you discover where your family was originally from and give you a new sense of heritage to be proud of.

Tracing Living Relatives

In addition to you finding out about ancestors, tracing your family tree can help you find living relatives all over the world. These extended cousins are part of your family and it is interesting making new ties.

If you are interested in tracing new living relatives then start with an ancestor, preferably one that produced many children or one that you find particularly intriguing (and double check that they are related to you first).

It might be easier to choose one with a unique name and before the mid-19th century providing the records are accurate. The process is quite simple. Using the same information to go backwards in time, you simply move forwards. Check your ancestor's records to find out the names and details of their children (this can be found in census records, marriage certificates, death certificates etc.) and by carrying on through one generation to the next, you will eventually discover a living relative.

Getting in Contact with a Living Relative

When you think you may have found a living relative you may want to get in contact and introduce yourself. What is the best approach? Firstly, even though you may be jumping up and down reaching for the phone and proclaiming, "Hi, I'm a distant relative of yours, fancy meeting up for coffee?", this is not a good idea. Nor is jumping in the car and turning up at their address uninvited.

Instead, in this digital age an email is the best way to go ahead. Write a friendly but casual message saying who you are, what you have found out and whether they would be interested in knowing more about the family tree. Perhaps ask them to confirm they received the email even if they don't want to know or want any further contact. A telephone number and address are good contact details to add.

If you are not technically minded or want a more personal approach, a hand-written letter is a good choice. You can explain what information you have discovered, how you discovered it and how you believe you are related.

It might be a good idea to include a copy of the family tree and perhaps copies of any old photographs as a visual representation can make people curious. Another good idea is to include a stamped address envelop so that they can write back to you or send you the chart and other documents back.

After this, be patient. Depending on where and when you send your letter, it could take a long time for it to reach them. Not only this, but some people can be hesitant in replying. They could want to double check what you have sent, talk to their family members and maybe even do a background check on you for safety purposes. Some take longer to pen a response.

If they respond to your initial letter, then there is the chance that the two of you will stay in contact. Perhaps after a period of time then you can talk on the phone, through email and/or eventually meet up in person.

Unfortunately, there are some who have zero interest in genealogy and may not want to get in contact with you. If you don't hear back from someone, do not continue getting in contact as sometimes people can be somewhat hostile. Just include any contact details and see if they have a change of heart further on down the road.

Organizing a Family Reunion

Should contact prove positive, eventually you may want to hold a family reunion. This needs to be organized well. Start by inviting family members a few months before the agreed upon date and to make sure they know to pass the information along to everyone in their family who is keen to go. Once you know roughly how many people want to attend, work out a budget and try to stick to it.

It might be a nice idea to choose a location that has a family tie – say, a village your ancestors lived in for generations. Make up an itinerary for the day as several events could help the family members, who are in fact strangers, to be more comfortable and sociable with everyone else. Maybe visit the churches where they were baptized, married or even buried. At the end of the day, a little family chart to give as a memento is a nice touch.

Conclusion

I want to thank you once again for purchasing this book and I hope you had a good read. The topic of DNA and genealogy has always been of utmost intrigue and scientific importance in modern times.

I hope the widespread information, from the basics of DNA to inheritance and its role in several diseases and conditions, was intriguing and informative.

I hope that through the medium of this book, you were able to satisfy your curiosity related to the subject of Genes and DNA.

Thank you and hope you had a good read.

RECOMMENDED READING

BODY LANGUAGE: How to Spot A Liar and Communicate Clearly

hyperurl.co/bodylang

AUTOIMMUNE DISEASE ANTI-INFLAMMATORY DIET

smarturl.it/autoa

NLP Subconscious Mind Power: Change Your Mind Change Your Life

hyperurl.co/NLP

Printed in Great Britain
by Amazon